Pra

The Changin

Retirement

MW01539548

"An excellent overview from 30,000 feet of the changing landscape of retirement. Mark outlines the common retirement mistakes and the unintended consequences of the mistakes. Developing, implementing and following the 'Retirement Roadmap' as discussed by Mark can assist in providing a stress-free retirement journey. This book is a must read for those entering or for those in the early stages of retirement."

David McMenamin, CFP®
Founder of Heritage Financial Services
(one of Tucson's leading retirement planning firms)

"For anyone hoping for a comfortable and confident retirement, Mark Singer's book is a must-read. It's packed full of great tips, lessons learned and information most of us never have a chance to obtain until it's too late. Whether you hope to retire, or are in retirement, you'll find something of value here."

Beverly Flaxington
Consultant, college professor and author of *Understanding Other People: The Five Secrets to Human Behavior*

"I found Mark Singer's book to be an interesting read. Chapter 4 (What About Women) is very enlightening regarding how women approach long-term financial security. Women do need help in focusing on their needs as opposed to putting everyone else's needs ahead of their own. Women need to think about their personal well-being first and foremost. The way Mark has written Chapter 4 hopefully will empower women to plan strategically on how to outlive their money.

"Now that Mark Singer has taken the first step to empower women to take charge, I hope there will be a second step to continue the process of helping women put themselves ahead of others and plan for their futures."

Darnell Frymire
Former CEO/Owner, The People Network, Inc. and
President, Community Affairs

"As a long-standing client of Mark Singer, I found The Changing Landscape of Retirement *to be a clear reflection of Mark's fundamental approach to always keeping the client at the center of the financial planning process. His personal and individualized approach to understanding his clients' needs and then developing a timely strategy to meet those needs has been clearly demonstrated to me many times over the nearly 20 years that we have been associated. Of particular interest was his chapter on how to choose a financial planner — I thought the material was very good and it is a topic that is seldom discussed so candidly.*

"This is a must-read for those seeking a successful retirement."

Fred Anderson
Retiree, Beverly, MA

"I would just like to thank you for empowering me with the knowledge that your book provided me. It forced me to ask myself some difficult questions for which in some instances I did not have the answers. Your book has however provided me with resources to seek those answers. The chapter on What About Women? also has opened my eyes and my mind. As a woman who owns a business but is also a wife, I developed some confidence after reading the chapter on What the Future Holds and understand that I really do not have to be afraid to ask the necessary questions that are needed in order to plan for my future financial needs. The book is an easy read, very informative and thought provoking. I would highly recommend this book and have already shared it with my three sisters."

Joanne L. Sargent, RN
Sargent & Associates Loss Management Services, Inc.

"It is written in a very accessible, friendly and understandable way. It isn't 'threatening' or overwhelming like lots of retirement books.

"It is very timely and current.

"I like the stories used to illustrate various points.

"[Mark Singer] very clearly underscores the importance of having a Retirement Roadmap."

Kathy Ridgely Beal, MBA
Director of Communications, American College of Medical Genetics

"As a woman so fittingly in the category Mark described as one who 'assumes the men in my life will take care of my investments and retirement planning for me,' I found this book to be eye-poppingly awakening!

"Not only did it make me more conscious of my financial outlook, but I found myself looking around and paying attention to what is important. It's not that the information in some cases isn't common sense, it's bringing it to the forefront of our brains and helping us be more alert and aware. I will definitely shift my financial perspective based on the facts presented."

Laurie Cote
President & CEO, Diversity Studio, Inc.

"As nearly 80 million Baby Boomers prepare to retire in the next 20 years, the adage that 'Those who fail to plan, plan to fail,' comes quickly to mind. But Baby Boomers are not the only ones who need to plan for retirement. People of all ages need to actively plan for their future if they hope to enjoy the comfortable retirement that so many of them dream about.

"In his new book, The Changing Landscape of Retirement, Mark Singer discusses the many items to be considered, and the major pitfalls to be avoided, in preparing for retirement. His 'Retirement Roadmap' also provides a planning tool that can be used in addressing the challenges that those who are approaching this next stage of life will face.

"Writing in an easy-to-read, conversational style, Mark illustrates many of his points with examples of real-life situations which he has encountered in his 25 years of helping people prepare for retirement.

"There's another old saying that goes, 'If you don't know where you are going, then how are you going to know when you get there?' By reading, and heeding, Mark Singer's The Changing Landscape of Retirement, today's Baby Boomers, and others, will be well-positioned to not only know where they are going, but to enjoy the retirement destination once they get there, as well."

Kurt Czarnowski
Former Regional Communications Director
for the Social Security Administration of New England

"Mark Singer's new book, The Changing Landscape of Retirement, is a must read for all women. This is the first book I have read that really shares with the reader the real troubles one can face when you don't plan. I love the real-life stories he shares in the book, which are helpful to understand the risks and rewards of planning properly for retirement. Mark understands what it takes to connect with women, the way they want to learn. His approach is supportive as a partner in retirement planning, not a vendor. I highly recommend Mark's new book as a tool for women of all ages to get the information they need to succeed in retirement planning!"

Janet Powers
Chief Executive Diva, Diva Toolbox™, LLC

The Changing Landscape of Retirement

What you don't know could hurt you.

Mark Singer CFP®

ATA Press

Published by ATA Press

ISBN 978-0-9837620-0-3

First printing: June, 2011

Table of Contents

FOREWORD

Diane Donovan
Editor, *Midwest Book Review*

M̲ark Singer has been involved in the financial planning business for over twenty-five years, and thus has observed many changes in the industry. During this time he's collected the stories of clients who have weathered many different business environments, but he's never seen as much confusion about options as in this current financial environment — and *The Changing Landscape of Retirement* reflects some of the new rules and approaches designed to promote more flexibility in retirement planning as a whole.

His is not a "one answer fits all" approach, but provides an important emphasis on keys to finding the types of answers that fit each reader's unique financial goals and perspective. As such it presents a method, not a formula — and this makes *The Changing Landscape of Retirement* more versatile than most retirement guides.

Money and lifestyle needs, sources of income streams and their different requirements, purchases and travel needs during retirement years, and other concerns all contribute to different "benchmarks" for retirement income goals. Financial decisions currently are too often based on fear rather than reality—fear of what adversely changing markets will do to retirement income streams.

Not planning for inflation and taking too much money from a retirement portfolio are only a few of the issues Mark Singer tackles in *The Changing Landscape of Retirement*. Add in the fact that retirement goals change over the decades but investment portfolios are often not adjusted to reflect these changes, and you have a conundrum that *The Changing Landscape of Retirement* addresses—the lack of flexibility and adjusted options and vision in retirement objectives.

New lessons geared to volatile, uncertain market conditions and changing consumer needs promote flexibility in vision and thinking, focusing on coordinating goals and understanding planning lessons key to retirement success. Chapters discuss changing scenarios which require redefining objectives, they show how to create a more flexible "Retirement Roadmap," and they tell how to coordinate paperwork and planning to achieve a unified yet movable set of objectives.

From special issues women face to selecting a financial planner or planning firm, this tells how to create a plan, coordinate different objectives, bring them all together, and then maintain a type of flexibility that can easily adjust to both changing markets and changing retirement goals.

Add in case history examples from Mark Singer's clientele and you have an outstanding, well-balanced survey highly recommended for business and consumer libraries seeking a successful strategy versatile enough to apply to a range of concerns.

INTRODUCTION

Charles Dickens wrote, "It was the best of times, it was the worst of times..." In my 25 years of experience in the financial services business, it seems that of late all we've really been experiencing are the worst of times. The stock market has been flat for a 10-year period; the headlines seem to indicate that we are going to be in a continued period of uncertainty and volatility, and for many, this means redefining what their ideal retirement was supposed to be.

In my recent interactions with clients, I have heard and seen a level of frustration that I have not seen since I first entered this business. And if my clients, who are as informed as any individuals through our proactive communications with them, are frustrated, then I can only assume that the masses are frustrated as well.

For 25 years I have been putting into my "book" file many of the experiences and stories that I have been witness to as president of a retirement planning firm. I never really knew when or if I would write the book. However, as a result of hearing over and over again the heightened level of frustration of those who are transitioning into retirement, or those recently retired, I felt that this was as good a time as any to address the changing landscape of retirement.

My objective for this book is not to write a timeless masterpiece but to address the mistakes, from both an investment and a planning perspective, that I see many people making in the current environment. Early in my career, when a problem arose, one of my first bosses instructed me to enter his office not only with the problem but with a solution as well. So I hope that I not only share with you some of the issues and concerns I've listened to, and mistakes I've seen people making, but also offer a different perspective on how to accomplish your retirement goals.

One of my favorite expressions, and I'm sure my staff will roll their eyes when they read this, is that I like to take a look at things from 30,000 feet. I intend to take the focus away from specific investment tips or asset allocation ideas and move the conversation to what is truly needed, which is to coordinate all the conversations with regard to retirement in such a way that you will know whether or not you are on the right track.

There is a wonderful quote from "Alice in Wonderland" that goes like this:

> "Would you tell me, please, which way I ought to go from here?"
> "That depends a good deal on where you want to get to," said the Cat.
> "I don't much care where—" said Alice.
> "Then it doesn't matter which way you go," said the

Cat.

"—so long as I get SOMEWHERE," Alice added as an explanation.

"Oh, you're sure to do that," said the Cat, "if you only walk long enough."

(*Alice's Adventures in Wonderland*, Chapter 6)

I am sure that we will all get somewhere if only we walk long enough. Unfortunately, in the world of retirement planning, without understanding exactly where it is you need to go and how you wish to go there, you may wind up in a place you did not intend to be in the first place. My hope is that when you finish this book, you will have a better sense of not only where you wish to be but how you would like to get there.

I offer you one final thought — and that is that there is no *one* right answer for everyone. What you are truly looking for is the right answer for *you*.

Several years ago, I had the opportunity to hear Yann Arthus-Bertrand at a conference I was attending. He was sharing with us a sampling of the hundreds of photographs he had taken for a book he had recently published called "Earth from Above." He told the story of going to a mountaintop in Switzerland and hoping to get a particular picture of some of the flowers that were on that mountaintop. When he got there, he found that the flowers he was hoping to photograph had lost their peak bloom as the result of a recent storm, and no longer represented the image he thought he was going to be taking. He told us he was disappointed that he was unable to get the photograph he had envisioned but then realized that if he just changed the angle from which he was taking the photograph, he could see the flowers from a whole different perspective. At that moment, he found the answer that was right for him, which was different than the answer he thought was right originally.

His message was that there is more than one right answer, and I hope you will find the answer that is right for you when you read this book.

If you do find solutions to your retirement planning questions in this book, I recommend that before you move forward that you consult your team of financial advisors.

INTERACTIVE WORKSHEETS

I've created a number of different worksheets that you can use to help apply the principles in this book to your own personal retirement journey. Just look for the icon shown to the left and then go to:

www.yourretirementjourney.com/worksheets

CHAPTER 1
MISTAKES

My Trip to Disney World

If you are like me, at some point your child or children were old enough that you took them to Disney World. My daughter was seven years old when I decided it was time that we go down to the land of wonder. Actually, what prompted me to go was that I had just attended an educational conference where one of the speakers was one of the senior marketing executives for Disney. He started out his session by asking those in the audience, and there were several hundred, how many had been to Disney World. Just about every hand in the room went up, except mine. So I figured it was time.

The first thing I did was take a look at the calendar and see where we could have an extended period of time to go down to Disney World; as it turned out, it was the Veteran's Day weekend during what happened to be the 25th anniversary celebration of Disney World. The next order of business was to go get The Book. You know what book that is: the book that tells you what rides to go to during what time of day and how long to expect to wait. Typically, I am not that much of a planner when it comes to these types of trips; however, it turned out to be one of the best investments I could make.

I did my research and found out which rides I should go on, and it absolutely made a tremendous difference in maximizing the time that we had in Disney World. So we spent less time in lines and more time having fun.

Another part of the research was finding out which airlines flew down to Orlando and how much it would cost. I also exercised extensive due diligence in reviewing the different types of accommodations, both on and off property, that would be suitable for our visit. We selected our flights, stayed on property at a wonderful resort, and ended up having the time of our lives. Upon my return, I created a book of memories that my daughter and I will cherish for many years to come.

So the question you may be asking is, why am I telling you about my Disney World trip?

The answer is that for most people the type of research and due diligence I spent in planning the trip to Disney World is more time and effort than they will spend planning for their retirement. Interestingly, planning for Disney World is not too unlike planning for your retirement.

When planning for the trip, we had to understand what our goals were. How much time were we going to spend? What was going to be our budget? How were we going to travel? Did we want to go by car or by plane? Do we want to go nonstop or save money and utilize a one-stop flight? Did

I want to spend premium dollars to get extra value from the resort where we would be staying? Did I want to spend as little money as possible on the accommodations, yet spend more money for a better dining experience? These were just some of the issues I had to deal with when planning the trip.

All of this planning centered on my objectives and the budget I had for my trip. It was not unlike the effort needed to set in place the planning necessary to pursue the retirement of my dreams. And, believe it or not, the questions are similar:

How much money do I need on a monthly basis to sustain the lifestyle I desire? How much income will be coming from my pension or Social Security? What type of travelling, family events, celebrations or purchases will be important during my journey into retirement? How much risk do I want to take with my portfolio? To whom do I want to leave my money when I die?

So, as you can see, there is research to be done whether you are planning your trip to Disney World or planning for your retirement journey. You need to set out what your objectives and goals are and understand the trade-offs of pursuing one avenue versus another.

The reason I started off this chapter with a story about Disney World is because I believe that the biggest mistake that most people make when it comes to their retirement is they do not plan for it. They take the same route as Alice in the story from "Alice in Wonderland," in which the cat tells Alice that surely she will get somewhere as long as she walks long enough. It may not be exactly where you wanted to get to, but you certainly get somewhere.

Knowing You Are On the Right Track

When my daughter was 15, she went on her first train ride alone. She was headed to a chorale rehearsal on the North Shore of Boston. She went to the train station and boarded the train. When the train started moving, I am sure that she was talking to those around her, because she likes to make friends with everyone. The conductor came up to her and asked her for her ticket, which she gladly handed to him. The conductor gave her the ticket back and said that he hoped she would have a good time in Boston.

Unfortunately for my daughter, the train she was on was going in the wrong direction.

She needed to be on the northbound train; however, she boarded the train going south. The reality is that she was on a train headed towards what she thought was her intended destination. Since this was her first time on the train alone, she was unaware of the fact that it was headed in the wrong direction. How was she to know; she had never done this before!

For many who are thinking about transitioning into retirement, this too is a first-time journey. And even though you may be headed towards "a destination," you may not know that it is not the "intended destination." *Many of us just don't know what we don't know, and therein lies a huge problem.*

If you don't know what questions to ask, and most don't, then it is very possible that you are on the southbound train when you were supposed to be headed north. It was easy for my daughter to get off the southbound train at the next stop and get onto the train headed in the right direction. The mistake that she made only meant that she was late for her chorale rehearsal. Unfortunately, some of the mistakes that you will make when planning for your retirement may not be so easily reconcilable.

It is very important to recognize what you don't know because, without this information, you may make mistakes that will undermine your definition of a successful retirement. Without the benefit of a properly designed Retirement Roadmap, you may be headed in the wrong direction.

The Retirement Roadmap

A Retirement Roadmap is a planning system that transitions your financial life from the Accumulation Stage (the working years) to the Distribution Stage (the retirement years).

It takes the mystery out of financial planning by answering the question "Can I do this, and do it when and how I want to?" The Retirement Roadmap asks the questions that help you navigate the deeper waters of retirement. The three most important questions it asks are:

· Are you and your spouse able to lead the retirement lifestyle you desire?
· Will your spouse be taken care of when you are gone?
· Have you adequately provided for your kids and for your family's legacy?

Proper Benchmarking

There is a popular advertising campaign that addresses the concept of knowing what your "retirement number" is. The first iteration of images was of people who were carrying around seven-figure numbers under their arms, smiling along the way to their destination, and then putting their "retirement numbers" in nice safe places.

With the market volatility, these images changed. At this point, you would see someone walking in the street with the number under his or her arm, and the number gets hit by the bus and falls to the street. That same person is in a restaurant where the number is set to the side and is subsequently set on fire as a result of the activities from the next table. Clearly the message had changed, indicating that there was now a rougher ride towards accomplishing your "retirement number."

The most recent image of this campaign is of an individual who is trimming the hedges, and above his head the words "gazillion bazillion" are in neon lights, symbolizing his "retirement number." When asked by his neighbor how he was going to accomplish his goal of achieving a gazillion bazillion dollars, the answer was that he was just going to continue to throw money as quickly as possible towards his retirement and see what happened.

This ad campaign has clearly been on target and has captured what many people have felt at various times: a sense of hopelessness and being jostled by markets that are volatile and uncertain. Clearly one of the messages from the sponsor of this ad campaign is that all you need to do is know what your number is and take care of it.

From my perspective, as cute as these ads are, they do not address some of the very real problems, and mistakes, that people have to be aware of.

The first issue is that most of the people carrying numbers under their arms had numbers that were well into seven figures. The numbers that reflected their "retirement number" were upwards of $1.4 to $1.7 million. In my experience, when

I tell somebody, either a client or a listener from one of my radio or television shows, that they have to accumulate upwards of $1.7 million in order to have their correct "number," there is usually a "deer in the headlights" look as a response. Few people truly recognize how to save enough money, given all of the day-to-day issues we all face, towards a goal that may be many years away.

I would submit that the message should have been not just what your number is, but how to discipline one's self to put away that kind of money. As important as knowing what "the number" is, is the understanding of what kind of risk we need to take and what time frame we have in order to accumulate the money necessary for our proper retirement nest egg.

The second issue I have with this ad campaign is that we don't tell people what to do once they have accomplished their goals. *One of the biggest mistakes I have found that most people make deals with this issue right here. Too many people continue to take more risk than is necessary with their investment portfolios, even after they have accomplished their "number," and end up losing a significant portion of their retirement nest egg, at just the wrong time.*

Many years ago, I spoke with an individual who was six months from retiring. He had enough saved in his retirement plan to create the desired retirement that he and his wife had dreamed of. That was the good news. The bad news was that his timing, and planning, could not have been worse. For this was in the late 1980s, and he was working for a very successful organization called Wang. He thought that as a result of having invested 100% of his retirement savings in Wang stock, he was a financial genius.

You know the rest of the story; two months before he was to retire, Wang stock dropped precipitously, devastating his retirement savings and rendering him unable to now pursue the retirement that he and his wife had dreamed of.

A couple of years ago, I met a woman who was preparing for her retirement. She was in her early 60s and was planning to retire within the next two to three years. The good news was that she had accomplished her number, and interestingly for her, her number was $1 million. The bad news was that neither she nor her broker knew what her number was. So what happened?

For all of her working life, she had been working with a series of brokers who had advised her to invest in such a way as to achieve as much growth as possible. While she was in her 30s and 40s, whether the market was going up or down was of little consequence because she had enough time to make up for a down market. Now, however, she was within a couple of years of retirement, and because she had achieved her number, which actually was the benchmark for her retirement success, it was necessary for her to change the investment objectives.

Because neither she nor her broker understood from 30,000 feet that she had actually accomplished her objectives, the portfolio remained with a growth orientation. In 2008, when the markets lost significant value, the $1 million portfolio dropped to $620,000, assuring that she could no longer retire as she had desired in two to three years.

It was not until after the markets had dropped in 2008 that we had the opportunity to speak. And it was not until then that she understood the importance of having a Retirement Roadmap and of successfully benchmarking the performance of the portfolio back to what her retirement objectives are. If she had understood the concept of the Retirement Roadmap, she would have changed the objectives for her investment portfolio to be geared more towards preservation than growth, potentially saving her portfolio tens of thousands of dollars in lost value. With a Retirement Roadmap, it would have been possible to retire according to her original plan. Without the Retirement Roadmap, she had no idea, nor did her broker, that she was headed in the wrong direction.

Mistakes

In this section, I will detail some of the mistakes that I have seen people make over the past 25 years. These mistakes seem to fall under two major categories, the first being planning mistakes and the second being mistakes made while investing. However, before we look at some of these mistakes, I think it is important to recognize a big issue that most people overlook, and that is the issue of how we deal with our emotions when planning for retirement.

The emotion that is most prevalent when I talk with people about their retirement is the feeling of great anxiety. Heading into the unknown, in this case retirement, can cause many sleepless nights. And while we lie awake at night wondering what lies ahead, we conjure up all sorts of scenarios where our planning could go awry.

The reason it is important to understand what emotions we are feeling is that typically emotion is the driving force behind our decision-making process. And if we are driven by our anxieties, our fear of the unknown, then it is possible that we will not be making the best choices for our futures.

The best example of making decisions based on fear is when we see those headlines in the newspaper, in the evening news or on the Internet that indicate that all or a part of the sky is going to fall down. Typically these headlines relate to market performance, and if the news is not good, then many are driven by panic to make changes to their investment portfolios. We all have been told that the worst time to make investment decisions is when we are driven by emotion (panic or fear), yet we cannot stop ourselves.

Will Rogers once stated, "I would rather have a return 'of' my money than a return 'on' my money." When we feel panic, we tend to revert to the feeling of just wanting to preserve our money in the short run, rather than continue to follow a well-crafted path of a balanced portfolio for the long run. This assumes that you have a well-crafted path, or a roadmap that you are actually following. For without this roadmap, it is much easier to allow your emotions to dictate the decision-making regarding your investment or retirement planning.

Another example of letting your emotions dictate your decision-making process is what I call the "fear of running out of money" syndrome. *Many of the people I have spoken to about retirement planning are fearful that if they spend money today, they will not have it available tomorrow. And this fear of running out of money becomes the primary force behind what you do, or do not do, in your retirement.*

If you are fearful of running out of money, you may not go on that trip you had dreamed of. You may cut back on the number of evenings you eat out with friends at restaurants. You cut back on the amount of money that you were going to give to your kids or grandkids. In other words, you end up not pursuing the retirement of your dreams but running from a retirement of your fears.

As we will talk about later in this book, the best way to overcome these fears is to have a Retirement Roadmap that can not only map out where you are supposed to go but also make a determination as to whether or not you are on track, and then make the necessary adjustments so that you stay on track. *The real benefit of a Retirement Roadmap is to take the mystery out of the decision-making process and to start making those decisions based on real fact, as opposed to being driven by the emotions of fear or anxiety.*

Planning Mistakes

Outliving Your Money

Several years ago, my mother got remarried. Her new husband's parents were still alive; Rose, who had become blind three years prior, was 97 years old, and Joe was 100. Rose and Joe had lived in the same house for almost 75 years, and one day Joe decided to go for a walk. Unfortunately, Joe could not figure out how to get back to the house. That was when the family decided Joe and Rose should enter a nursing home. So the family searched for a nursing home that would accommodate Joe and Rose's wish to be in the same room with separate beds.

One endearing part of this story happened the very first night that Joe and Rose were in the nursing home; Rose said to Joe that he should stay in his own bed because the beds they now had in the home were smaller than the beds they had in their own home. Having been married for so long, Joe was not about to sleep alone and joined his wife for that first night in the home.

Joe and Rose were unable to attend the actual wedding ceremo-

PLANNING MISTAKES

- Outliving Your Money
- Not Planning for Inflation
- Taking Out Too Much Money
- Not Working with a Specialist
- Beneficiary Forms
- IRA Rollover Mistakes
- Having Too Many Accounts
- The Transition Into Retirement
- Not Understanding Time Frames

ny for my mother and their son. So after the ceremony, about a dozen of us drove an hour north to the nursing home to reenact the wedding ceremony for Joe and Rose. My daughter, who at the time was about 13, stood next to Rose and did a play-by-play announcement for Rose, since she was unable to see, of the ceremony at hand. There wasn't a dry eye in the house.

I tell you this story not because I want you to know Joe and Rose but to give you an indication of something that you already know: We are living longer. The hope is that we are not only living longer, but that we are living better and more quality lives as well. The paradigm shift is that we must now plan to be living into our 90s, unless some indication of poor health suggests otherwise.

Hopefully, the good news is that we are living longer and are leading better lives at later ages, allowing us to maximize the joy of the retirement journey. However, if you make bad assumptions while putting in place your Retirement

Roadmap and these assumptions are compounded over a 30- or 35-year period, then your plan is not going to be worth the paper it is written on.

One of the biggest mistakes that I find people make when dealing with the issue of longevity is that the assumptions they use with the boilerplate plans available on the Internet or through some of their brokers are not reflective of reality. The problem here is that when you compound out bad assumptions over a long period of time, the foundation for the plan that you have is poor at best. Many times people input these initial assumptions but never revisit them in subsequent years to make necessary adjustments to the plan. The result of this is that the plan no longer reflects market reality, the economy or one's own life.

Again, the good news is that we could potentially live longer, but we cannot use today's assumptions and expect that they will remain the same five, 10 or 25 years from now. So those who are going to put together their own Retirement Roadmap must remember to make proper assumptions and to make no less than annual evaluations of whether or not they are still on the right track for their retirement.

Not Planning for Inflation

One of the big mistakes I find people make is assuming that whatever is happening today should be used as their assumption for the next X years to come. One of those variables that is used within planning modules is inflation.

Historically, inflation has run at about a 4 to 4.5% rate per year. However, the recent inflation numbers, if you believe them, are near the 2 to 2.5% rate. So if you are going to put in place assumptions for your retirement, and you use today's inflation rate and then have that compounded for the duration of the plan, your plan will blow up.

When I run Retirement Roadmaps for clients, I input the historical inflation rate. This creates a margin of error that I am comfortable with. I would much rather have more money than less. If I put in an inflation rate that is higher than the current rate and make the adjustments annually looking forward, then I build a more conservative plan for my client.

Let me share with you an example of the type of poor planning that this could cause when inputting and compounding the wrong inflation rate.

Let's say, for example, the initial plan indicates that the client needs $100,000 annually in order to accomplish their retirement objectives. If we put in place a 2.5% inflation rate and compound that over the next 25 years, the $100,000 need becomes a $185,000 need in 25 years. If, however, we put in a 4% inflation rate and compound that over the same timeframe, that need grows to $266,000 per year.

There is a substantial difference in planning for those two future numbers. I would rather solve for the $266,000 need in 25 years, and potentially be short of that goal if necessary, versus solving for the $185,000 need and being short of *that* goal.

One of my passions is golf, and I have heard many times that an amateur golfer will assume he or she will hit the perfect shot with a fairway iron. This assumption is usually incorrect; we do not hit the perfect shot and therefore usually fall short of the intended target. This thought process, I find, is the same for those who plan for retirement.

They assume that everything will work perfectly and put in

place a plan that has no margin for error. The golfer should take one extra club and the planner should be putting in assumptions that are just a little higher, or bring margin for error into the plan.

Taking Out Too Much Money

Another common mistake I have found that people make, and this applies to both do-it-yourselfers and too many of my peers in this industry, is to take out too much income from their investment portfolios.

Several years ago, I was talking to a prospective client who mentioned that he had just had a plan done through a well-known Boston firm. He explained that he gave the adviser all of his information, needs, objectives and goals in an effort to generate a plan that was reflective of an investment portfolio for his upcoming retirement.

This prospective client was thrilled that he was going to be able to accomplish his retirement objectives because the plan indicated that he would get a 7% income from the portfolio, enough to lead his desired lifestyle. *This* plan was not reflective of what we would call prudent planning.

Current studies indicate that a withdrawal rate of approximately 4% is the maximum amount one should take from the portfolio if one's goal is not only to create an income stream but also to preserve the asset base. So when this individual stated he was going to take 7% income from the portfolio, what he did not realize was there was going to be a trade-off — his income would last for a period of time and he would then run out of money.

One of the mistakes I find when talking with people is that

they confuse the concept of taking income with the concept of a stock or mutual fund generating a dividend for its shareholders. So let me take a moment to share with you how to properly think about how to take income from a portfolio.

Investment vehicles, like stocks, bonds or mutual funds, can have what is called a "total return." This return is made up of income, oftentimes the yield or dividend produced plus any capital appreciation that may be earned by the particular investment. For this discussion, I will keep it simple and not worry about whether the account is taxable or nontaxable.

Traditionally, when individuals think of income, they think of the dividend or the yield that is generated by the investment. For planning purposes, we often think of income in a little bit of a different way.

So let's move up to 30,000 feet and take a look at a hypothetical planning scenario. We will assume that the client needs $100,000 of income to accomplish her retirement goals, and she has pension and Social Security income of $70,000 per year. This leaves her $30,000 short, meaning that the investment portfolio needs to throw off $30,000 worth of income. We will assume for this purpose that there is $1 million in the investment portfolio; therefore, this portfolio needs to distribute 3% of the assets in order to accomplish the desired goal.

From a planning perspective, I do not care whether the 3% comes from dividends or capital appreciation. Our goal is to generate $30,000, and it is not a concern (again, ignoring taxes) how it is generated.

Assuming the client needs to generate 3% income and that we are having to overcome a 4% inflation rate looking forward, the portfolio needs to have a total return, for planning purposes, of 7%. If the portfolio can generate a 7% long-term total return, we will be able to generate the 3% income now and also account for the impact of inflation, annually, looking forward. (I am not suggesting here that a 7% total return should be expected or is historically accurate; I am just using it hypothetically to show how to think about total return and how to withdraw money from one's investments.)

Not Working with a Specialist

We are blessed, in the Boston area, to have some of the best medical care available in the nation. Along with having some of the best care, we have some of the best and most noted experts to help us out when it comes to specific ailments. So when I have a problem with my shoulder as a result of playing many years of tennis, I seek out a medical professional who has dealt with not only shoulder issues, but shoulder issues specific to those who have played sports.

I could go to a general practitioner who has years of experience in the medical profession and is well-versed in all of the latest remedies. He may be someone who is well respected and highly regarded, but is not an expert when it comes to shoulder issues for those who played tennis. This does not mean that he is not good at his craft; it just means that this professional is not the proper professional for my specific needs.

This analogy holds true when seeking out a professional to help guide you through your retirement planning. (In Chapter 5, we will explore in much more detail what to look for when looking for a specialist. My objective here is to open your eyes so that you are aware that there are actually retirement planning specialists.)

A study was done several years ago by a well-named mutual fund company. The objective was to find out how individuals sought advice for their planning needs and how they made decisions during their working years. As part of the study, the individuals surveyed were asked questions about planning for retirement and how their behavior may have changed, along with their decisions about their financial advisers, as they got closer to the actual date of retirement.

The conclusion of this study was that during their working years the average couple engages 2½ financial advisers. These advisers could be defined as brokers, life insurance agents or anyone else offering financial advice. However, as the couple approached retirement, they felt the need to get advice from just one "go to" financial advisor who specialized in the retirement process.

It is important from a consumer's perspective to understand how financial advisors are trained and educated. There are many different types of advisors, some of whom are generalists and others are specialists. To understand this better, I share with you my road over the past 25 years of gaining the knowledge, education and training that I needed along the path to becoming a retirement planning specialist.

For many who enter our industry, it is important to find an organization that will provide broad training and a track to run on in an effort to help us gain the experience and expertise needed to deal with the public. My very first experience in the financial planning industry was through Mutual of New York life insurance. Twenty-five years ago, the life insurance industry taught the very basics of financial planning and how to market your services and go get business.

The time I spent with Mutual of New York was worthwhile because it gave me an understanding of financial planning 101. For that I will be forever grateful. But as Harry Chapin once wrote about a little town in upstate New York, he "felt he spent a week there one day." I sort of felt the same way about my time in the life insurance industry. There were certainly some benefits to learning the grassroots of financial planning, but I did not see selling life insurance as the way I wished to further my career as a financial planner.

I then decided to move out on my own, and share office space with three other financial planners. The decision to go out on my own right out of the gate was both the best and the worst career decision that I have made. For without a track to run on, without guidance from an organization, I was left all on my own to learn all of the complexities, not only of the financial planning profession, but also of building a business as a sole proprietor. These were the toughest times, yet as a result of this career path decision, they certainly helped me become what I am today.

Starting out on my own, I learned how to become a financial planning generalist. I became knowledgeable in the many aspects of financial planning, including life insurance, investments, taxes, estate planning and much more. About seven years after I made the decision to go out on my own, I stepped back one day to evaluate where I was and where I would like to go. What I realized was that the number one concern of many of my clients was the issue of retirement, and that I had developed some of the insight necessary to start my way toward becoming a retirement planning specialist.

Many of my peers stayed the course as either life insurance

agents or financial planning specialists, and have done very well for themselves. I am glad that I have taken the road to becoming a retirement planning specialist, because it has been very rewarding, both personally and professionally, to work with the clients of my firm for over 20 years.

I share the story of the journey of my professional development because I think it is important to recognize that there are many good professionals out there. As you decide to work with a financial professional, you will need to determine what the best fit is for you and your family (more on this in Chapter 5).

As a retirement specialist, one of the most frequently asked questions by those about to retire is "When I retire, how will I get the income I will need?"

There are two distinct phases of financial planning. The first is the accumulation stage. Typically, during your working years, your goal is to accumulate the largest retirement nest egg possible so that you may have the opportunity to retire with the lifestyle you desire. However, when you start to transition into retirement, you now enter the distribution stage. This stage focuses on positioning the portfolio so that you can generate the income you need in the most tax-efficient manner for retirement now, and later.

In addition to this change of perspective, the conversations change as well. During the accumulation stage, the primary focus is on putting as much money away as possible so you can achieve the highest value possible. The topic of money management is often the primary focus of the conversations with your broker. Once you start to move into the distribution stage, the issue of money management becomes only one of many important topics to be discussed with your retirement planner. It is the ability to coordinate and sync up all of the various issues, including but not limited to income generation, estate planning, tax efficiencies, preservation of assets, and money management, that make the distribution stage a more focused and complex area within the world of financial planning.

So I believe that as important as it was for me to find a shoulder specialist in order to get the right treatment, it is important for you to align yourself with a specialist who can deal with your particular financial issues.

Beneficiary Forms

Several years ago, I was talking to a prospective client who was about to retire from GE. Joe walked into my office with all of the paperwork we had asked him to bring in for the interview. We proceeded to review his goals and objectives for his upcoming retirement. About 30 minutes into the interview, I told Joe that even if I could get him the returns he was looking for, his entire retirement plan was going to go up in smoke.

You can find a beneficiary review worksheet on our website (see introduction for details).

One of his goals was to leave his retirement nest egg to his two children. However, as I reviewed the documents, I noticed that the beneficiary of his 401(k) plan was his ex-wife. The divorce had occurred over 25 years ago, yet Joe never went back and updated the beneficiary form. I see this mistake often, and it is a fundamental reason why so many plans are going to fail.

I cannot tell you how many times I have seen a name that should not be on the beneficiary form, either because Aunt Molly passed away 12 years ago or because there was a divorce. Regardless of the cause, the objectives for the planning are no longer properly reflected in the documents necessary to distribute the assets. *I believe incorrect beneficiary forms are one of the biggest reasons individuals will not accomplish their overall retirement goals.*

Oftentimes you don't even know what you don't know. In this case, not understanding the impact of an incorrect beneficiary designation form will be the downfall from a planning perspective. Up-to-date and accurate beneficiary designation forms will help you avoid this mistake, as well as put in place the potential of maximizing the value of an IRA through what is called a Stretch IRA designation.

The IRS allows you to distribute income to your surviving spouse and the next two generations. When done properly, there is the potential of turning a $100,000 IRA into a $1 million stream of income to your heirs. But without designating the proper beneficiaries, you will not be able to utilize the Stretch IRA concept once you are gone.

By properly coordinating your investment strategies with your estate planning desires, the Stretch IRA can become one of the most powerful tools when instituting your Retirement Roadmap.

IRA Rollover Mistakes

In my 25 years of experience, one of the planning areas where I have seen many mistakes made, and many of them very costly, is with the rollover of an IRA. Here is just one example of how costly a mistake could be if the planning is done incorrectly.

Non-spousal IRA rollovers, defined as rollovers to one who

is not a spouse, have become a main source of confusion for both individuals and some of their financial advisors. Several years ago, a prospective client came to me after having received advice from a local bank's financial planning division. Fortunately for this person, she did not completely trust the information that she had just received and decided to come to me for a second opinion. This second opinion ended up saving her almost $250,000.

The situation involved an IRA she had inherited from her father, who had recently passed away. The IRA was worth almost $600,000, and she was the sole beneficiary of the account. The advice that she had received from the bank's advisor was to set up a rollover IRA account in her name, and have a check from the old account be sent directly to her so that she could bring the check into the bank to deposit in the new IRA.

There were two glaring mistakes that the bank's advisor had made. First, a non-spousal rollover can only be transacted with a trustee-to-trustee transfer. If this individual had actually executed the request for the "check," the transaction would have instantly and irreconcilably been deemed a full distribution from the IRA and therefore fully taxable. The only way to make a "transfer" for a non-spousal IRA rollover is with a trustee-to-trustee transfer, which by definition means no "check" is needed. It is actually just a wire transfer from one account to the other.

The second error made by the bank advisor was that she was instructed to open her own IRA rollover account. It is important when doing rollovers to title the account properly, and in this instance the new account had to be designated as a beneficiary or BDA rollover. Without the proper designation, the rollover, by IRS regulations, is not correct and could be subject to substantial taxes.

Another error that is made with non-spousal rollovers is the lack of understanding that the beneficiary, in this case the recipient of the IRA, must initiate required distributions according to the IRS actuarial tables (or exhaust the balance within 5 years). To make matters more confusing, the level of distributions will be different depending upon the decedent's age at passing and whether he/she had already begun to take out their required minimum distributions.

The lesson here is that you should be double-checking the advice you receive regarding rollovers with a specialist. A mistake in planning could potentially cost you a lot of money.

Having Too Many Accounts

Throughout life's journey, we tend to accumulate things, and this holds true when it comes to accumulating money. I had a client recently who came in with no fewer than 15 different accounts. He had joint accounts in three different banks, taxable investment accounts with two different investment companies, annuities with three different insurance companies, and three different IRAs with two different financial advisors.

There are several issues, from a planning perspective, with having too many accounts. The first issue is that there are so many statements with so much paperwork coming in so frequently that, more often than not, you never truly know what exactly it is that you own. With so much paperwork, many people actually feel out of control. They sort of bury their heads in the sand and hope it will all magically get done.

The second issue is if you don't really know everything that you own, how can you properly put together an investment portfolio that is well diversified? When we started to compile and coordinate all of the different accounts, the client kept coming up with more paperwork for more accounts, revealing more and more funds that they owned and had not accounted for originally. It was almost impossible to put together a coordinated and well-balanced investment portfolio.

The third issue is tax efficiency. If you cannot get a handle on exactly how the income is coming in, because you don't know all of the accounts that you have, how do you take control of the "income faucet?" Once you enter into retirement, not only do you need to generate income but you need to generate it tax-efficiently. The "income faucet" refers to the ability to turn on and off the income when you need it. If you are unaware of all of the accounts you own, and the only accounting for the income is when you bring all of the paperwork to your accountant, then you are probably paying more taxes than you should.

A fourth issue is if the paperwork is too overwhelming and you do not look at correspondence in a timely fashion, you are probably unaware of updates to portfolios, money manager updates and new product enhancements that could potentially help you accomplish your retirement goals.

Finally, when you get to the age when you are required to take minimum distributions from your IRAs, yet you are not sure where all of the IRAs are, then you may be subjecting yourself to one of the IRS's heftiest penalties. The penalty for not taking out enough when you are beyond the age of 70½ is 50% of the amount that should have been taken out. Each custodian of your IRA is mandated to send you correspondence indicating how much money should be distributed from the IRA account each year. If you have six or eight different IRA accounts, you are going to be getting six or eight custodial letters every single year. Why not consolidate this so you don't get more than two or three of these letters, removing some of the confusion with regard to required minimum distributions?

I believe in the KISS theory, whereby simpler is better. By consolidating accounts where possible, you gain more control over the investments and the information flow, which should help you gain more control with your retirement planning.

The Transition Into Retirement

From a planning perspective, I think it is important to address what you will be doing in retirement. We have talked so far about what your money will be doing when you retire; however, one of the biggest mistakes I find people make is not thinking through what their retirement will look like.

We go to work for many different reasons. It is not just the paycheck. Work provides us with a reason to get up in the morning, a place to go, interaction with other people, a sense of achievement or purpose, and much more. So when you leave the workforce, you will be leaving many of your friends and a big part of what had defined you for many years. It is crucial to the success of your journey into retirement that you step back, before you retire, to understand what your retirement will look like.

Oftentimes when we talk to a husband about his retirement, his wife will go off and gain employment (if she was not already employed) because she really doesn't want to see him for those extra 40 to 50 hours every workweek. Sit down with your spouse and/or family and have a long conversation about what you wish to accomplish once you leave the workforce. What passions do you have? What hobbies will you explore? Are there grandkids that you will be babysitting for (this happens to be the favorite hobby of one of my clients)?

You should take on this task at least one year before you expect to retire. Obviously, if you have been retired involuntarily, you will be unable to undergo this task before retirement; however, it is still important to properly plan retirement just as you would have if you had the option to retire voluntarily.

The retirement journey is driven by many factors, not the least of which is the economics. However, many of my clients define a successful retirement with the following statement: "I don't know how I had enough time to work before!" They are so busy during the working years that the successful retirement is defined by what they are doing, not what their money is doing for them. Certainly these two will go hand-in-hand when defining a successful retirement, and you must spend the proper time doing the necessary planning.

Not Understanding Time Frames

The journey towards retirement can be very complex. One issue I find many people don't understand is the issue of time frames. I mentioned previously in this chapter the individual who was going to retire from Wang.

Clearly, he did not understand planning for the proper time frame; if he had, he would not have taken the risk associated with having 100% of his retirement savings in company stock so close to the date of retirement (hopefully this is a mistake you will never make, regardless of the organization you are working for). When you get closer to retirement, it is important to understand how to benchmark your retirement goals (also discussed earlier in this chapter).

Typically, we find people take a serious look at retirement when they are about five to seven years away from their perceived retirement date. Once they set up their Retirement Roadmap, they will understand what their benchmark numbers are and, therefore, what to do with their investments. The closer you get to your retirement date, if you have accomplished your benchmark number, the more important it is that you go into a conservative investment mode rather than maintaining a growth mode. If the market drops significantly and you don't have enough time to make up for it, you may never be able to accomplish your retirement benchmark number again if you are too close to your retirement date.

I am not suggesting that when you retire, the management of your money should retire. You should be aligning the management of your money with your retirement goals, which will be discussed in a future chapter. I am suggesting, however, that you should be aware of where you are on the journey to retirement and making the appropriate investment decisions as a result.

This is no different than if you were looking at your investment portfolio as it related to your children and funding their college educations. When those kids get closer to the age of 18, the management approach of the college monies should be getting more and more conservative. If your kids are three and five, you can afford to take on significant risk because you have significant time ahead of you to make up for market declines. The philosophy is the same when it comes to your retirement planning.

Without a Retirement Roadmap and without proper benchmarking, you will never be able to get a handle on when to move the switch from growth to conservative within your portfolio, nor understand how well that money is being managed against your retirement goals. The roadmap becomes a crucial part of the planning for your retirement, and without it, mystery will continue to shroud many of your investment decisions.

Investment Mistakes

The Definition of Insanity

The definition of insanity is doing the same thing over and over again and expecting different results. In my 25 years of business, I have spoken to many people who fall into this category. More often than not, the scenario plays out like this: the markets go up, and you put more money into them. The markets go down, and you panic and take money out. And somehow when the market goes up again, you put more money into them, repeating the scenario over and over again and never truly learning from the previous mistakes.

INVESTMENT MISTAKES

· Having All Your Eggs in One Basket
· Asset Allocation
· Not Rebalancing
· Not Diversifying Properly
· Not Understanding Risk

The markets that we are experiencing right now are

different than markets we experienced in the '80s and '90s, and if there is not an understanding of what the difference is, you will continue to make the same mistakes over and over again.

It is important to understand that when I reference "markets," I am referring to long-term trends. For the purpose of this discussion, I am not concerned about the daily, weekly or even annual returns of the market. Unfortunately, when individual investors and/or brokers are reviewing market performance, they do tend to look at it with a sort of a tunnel vision, unable to see the big picture from 30,000 feet.

During the '80s and '90s the long-term trend, which ended up being one of the greatest bull markets in history, was that the markets could sustain upward momentum. However, since 2000, we have been unable to sustain upward movement and have been in a flat market for the past 10 years. If you are looking at your quarterly statements and using those statements and/or the most recent headlines or news events to determine your next move with your investments, then you are bound to continue to make mistakes.

It is interesting to note the differences in expectations of individual investors during these two different time frames. I vividly recall a conversation I had with a prospective client in the late 1980s when this individual came in expecting returns over the following 10 years of somewhere between 18% and 20% per year. My response to him at the time was that I thought his expectation levels were too high and he was going to be taking on too much risk, and I was unwilling to take on the task of helping him manage his money if those were his expectations.

In stark contrast to that conversation is the conversations I have on an ongoing basis with individuals today. Expectations for the long term have dropped to numbers closer to 5% or 7%, and even those numbers seem at times to be unrealistically high. The reality is that the actual number is probably somewhere between each of these two conversations.

From 30,000 feet, it is clear that the long-term trends have changed, that they may continue to move in this direction for another few years to come, and your investment decisions need to be driven by this paradigm shift (I will detail this more in Chapter 2).

There are certainly no guarantees when it comes to investing, but without doing proper due diligence beforehand, your probability of achieving your investment goals could decline.

Having All Your Eggs in One Basket

This is a mistake driven by not only an error in judgment with your investments, but also a false sense of security if you work for one large organization. I see this happen often, and its effects can be disastrous.

I have already referenced the scenario with the Wang employee. He had worked at Wang his entire career, and his judgment with regard to investment decisions was clouded at best. He obviously felt that since he had worked at Wang for many years, "they" would take care of him when he retired. He had benefited greatly from the growth of the stock for many years and, as a loyal employee, was sure that this growth would continue. *This "blind faith" in one's company can potentially be the single most costly mistake one could make heading into retirement.*

If you work, or worked, for Polaroid, Enron, General

Electric, Goldman Sachs, BP or any other large organization whose stock fell precipitously at just the wrong time, you clearly understand the risk. No matter how long you have worked for an organization and no matter how well you think you know the business model and how the stock performs, it is never a prudent choice to invest heavily in that one stock.

Recalling many conversations I have had with individuals who had up to 100% of their employer stock within their 401(k) program, it is interesting to hear people talk about their investment philosophy. Many times they will tell me that they are conservative when it comes to their investment philosophy, and it is important to understand what is meant when they say this.

"Conservative" here means that they are very familiar with, or feel very comfortable with, their own organization. They have been loyal employees and feel that no matter what happens, the company will take care of them.

When I question someone who has 100% of their investment portfolio in their employer's stock, I get a number of different responses. First, there is the response that indicates that they are well aware of the risk that they are taking but that the company's growth is still targeted to be outstanding for the next several years, and they don't want to miss out on that.

Next there is the individual who has been with an organization, such as General Electric, where the stock used to be at $60, dropped to $30 and then to $20, and that individual is waiting for the stock value to go back up to the previous valuations before they consider selling. This assumes the stock is going to go back up. Again, there was a "blind faith" that the stock was going to take care of them and certainly would be going up, not down.

Then there is the response from the soon-to-be retiree that they recognize they are overweight in the portfolio, completely dependent upon the value of that stock in order to accomplish their retirement goals, and would not have it any other way.

To these folks, I could get on the top of the mountain and declare that I have the cure for all that ails them, and still not be heard. There is little I can do to sway someone emotionally who has been employed as long as many have been with one company. No matter how intelligent these people are in other areas of life, they are putting themselves in harm's way, and I can only wish them well.

Unfortunately, for these folks who are hoping not to miss out on future gains, they do not realize that the potential losses could be much more detrimental to their retirement than any gain may benefit them.

For those who recognize the pitfalls of taking this type of investment risk, particularly as one approaches the five- to seven-year window before their retirement date, I can share with them how to properly diversify the portfolio, take on the appropriate risk, and sync up their investment philosophy with their retirement goals.

Recently, I was talking with someone who was five years from his retirement date. He works for one of the largest worldwide organizations, has been there for 35 years, and is anxiously looking to retire comfortably. He, like many of his peers, had upwards of 95% of his investments in his 401(k) plan in his corporate stock.

When we first took on the task of putting together his

Retirement Roadmap, I mentioned to him that one of the issues we were going to have to deal with was his current investment strategy. He knew exactly where I was going with this comment and made it clear that at that moment he was not willing to discuss the possibility of diversifying his holdings.

Once we completed his Retirement Roadmap and there was an understanding that he could accomplish his retirement goals, even with modest returns, we decided to revisit the conversation about investments. Since we had taken a different path to understanding how to retire, he was more aware of what he needed to do to retire comfortably. In his case, he was fortunate enough to have already accumulated enough money to successfully retire.

Now that we had established he had achieved his "benchmark" number for his desired retirement and that it was no longer necessary to achieve "outstanding" returns, he was willing to revisit the overall allocation within his 401(k) plan. By taking a different perspective and doing the Retirement Roadmap first, before we took a look at how to diversify his portfolio, he was more empowered and knowledgeable about both the upside and downside of the journey into retirement.

This goes back to synchronizing your investment portfolio with your retirement goals. During our working years, we are looking to accumulate as much money as possible, yet no one has told us when, or how, to make the necessary change once we have accomplished our goals. And that is assuming that you actually have goals. *Learn the lessons of history. Don't let how you feel about your tenure at your organization drive you to make poor investment decisions that could potentially derail a successful retirement.*

When I did retirement planning seminars, I would ask the audience the following question: "What is the most important characteristic of putting together an investment portfolio?" The answer, invariably, was that the most important consideration from the audience's perspective was the selection of the "best" investment or fund manager. This was typically the answer from the do-it-yourselfers in the room, as well as those who were using financial planners.

The do-it-yourselfers would spend significant amounts of time researching specific investments and selecting these investments based on their research. Those who used financial planners were also convinced that the selection process of investment managers was the most important characteristic, because that was the embodiment of the majority of the conversations they had with their financial advisors.

To reinforce our perception of how important it is to select the best managers or investment vehicles, television shows, talking heads on radio shows and prominent magazines would annually, if not more frequently, list their top 50 picks. Interestingly, many of these picks rarely made it to the next set of top picks, which meant that the resource that you were using was asking you to churn your portfolio no less than every year. From a planning perspective, this is never prudent advice.

There was a study done many years ago, authored by Harry Markowitz. Markowitz was honored with a Nobel Prize in economics in 1990. He had been studying markets since the late 1940s in a search for what was the most important factor for the growth of a portfolio. This study has become the landmark study for our industry and how we look at portfolio construction.

Markowitz's study looked at several contributing factors to a portfolio's total return, including the impact of timing, investment selection, taxes/fees and asset allocation. The conclusion from this study was that over 90% of the success of an investment portfolio was driven by asset allocation.

Let me repeat that asset allocation contributed, according to Markowitz, to over 90% of the success of markets over many years. Timing, selection of individual managers or investment vehicles, and taxes/fees contributed to less than 10% of the overall total return of the portfolio. Obviously, this is contrary to the perceptions of individual investors and many of my peers in the industry.

The decision-making process about asset allocation during long-term secular bear markets, markets that have basically no return from the beginning of the cycles to the end of the cycles, like the one we are in now, is different than asset allocation decisions we would make during long bull markets like the ones we saw in the '80s and '90s.

Suffice it to say that the investment community and many of my peers need to be reeducated about what is the most important component with regard to putting in place a proper investment portfolio. *It is much more important to put in place the proper asset allocation than it is to have the "best" investment vehicle.*

Not Rebalancing

Can you think back far enough and remember the late 1990s from an investment perspective? The technology sector was going crazy; we kept hearing of this "new normal" where it was more important, it seemed, to lose money than it was to show earnings. Many of the big-name tech stocks were skyrocketing in value with seemingly no end in sight.

The mistake made was not so much believing in this fairytale as it was not getting back to investment basics. Within your portfolio in the early '90s, you may have started out with growth or technology funds that represented maybe 25% to 35% of your portfolio. By the end of the 1990s, the monies in this sector, due to extraordinary growth, had risen to 60%, 70% or even 80% of your portfolio.

In essence, we fell in love with the technology sector and forgot about the investment basics which indicated that at some point you needed to rebalance. The investment portfolios that you had were so out of balance as a result of the extraordinary growth of the technology sector that you put yourself in harm's way. The assumption here is that we actually had an investment policy statement to go by.

An investment policy statement (IPS) would outline an appropriate balancing process for the portfolio. This is important because, as sectors rise and fall, you need to buy or sell various sectors to bring the overall portfolio back to proper balance. At some point, as the technology/growth sectors started to represent over 50% of your portfolio, a systematic approach to selling would have been indicated by the IPS. If you had the proper parameters and the discipline to make the necessary changes as you became out of balance over time, you would have saved yourself and your portfolio the degree of loss many suffered. Certainly, there are no guarantees for any future or past performance.

In secular bear markets, such as the one we are experiencing right now, it is more important than ever to have a proper IPS in place. *Due to the volatility of these markets, it is imperative to have the guidelines necessary to know how your investments should be situated, and how to make the necessary adjustments when the markets change swiftly, which is what we are experiencing currently.*

It is not unusual, as I talk with people, to hear them tell of their mistakes of buying high and selling low. They usually chuckle when they think of how they go about the investment process. The interesting thing is that if you had systematic changes programmed into your investment portfolio, the process of buying high and selling low could be avoided because you would be taking the emotions, or panic, out of your investment decisions.

It is important not to fall in love with your investments. Do the research necessary to bring in place the proper asset allocation and weightings necessary to accomplish your retirement objectives, and then go out and find very good managers who fit into your investment approach.

Not Diversifying Properly

It is not uncommon, when a prospective client comes into my office and shares with me what they own within their portfolios, to see a very common mistake: he or she owns too many funds doing the same thing. Typically when I point this out, I am told by this individual that he or she really is very well diversified. I point out to him or her that even if you had CDs in eight different banks, you would not be bringing more diversification in; you would just have eight different CDs.

There are somewhere between 15,000 and 20,000 mutual funds available. There are many different sectors that are offered through the mutual funds, and hundreds of different funds offering the same type of investment style within each category. So when a prospective client comes in and is proud of the fact that he or she has a well-balanced portfolio with 15 mutual funds in it, he or she may be a bit taken aback if he or she was to find out that of the 15 mutual funds, 10 of them were investing in the same space.

It is not always possible, just by looking at the label of the mutual fund, to actually find out what it is they own. Sometimes you really have to dig into the prospectus or the available research to find out what the managers can, and do, invest in. If you have 10 different large-cap growth domestic mutual funds, then you do not have the type of diversification and balance that you may have expected originally.

Again, it is sort of like having CDs in eight different banks. Not all of them will be doing exactly the same thing as the others, yet they will typically be drawing from the same basket of stocks or bonds, and the holdings for the funds would have tremendous overlap.

The goal, therefore, is not to own a lot of funds or stocks; rather, own the correct amount of investment vehicles that coordinate well with each other in order to be balanced properly.

Not Understanding Risk

Let us take a moment to address the definition of risk. When I conduct speaking engagements and ask the audience about its definition of risk, typically the answer comes back that risk is about the potential of losing money. And most people would prefer not to lose money; therefore, they make decisions not to take on "risk."

So let us redefine for you what risk is relative to your retirement planning and your investment portfolio. If you take on more risk than you should, you run the "risk" of losing more money than you should. This is the scenario with my client who had $1 million, took on more risk than she should have, given how close she was to retirement, and ended up losing "too much money." However, it is also possible not to take on "enough risk." What do I mean by that?

If your Retirement Roadmap indicates that you need to generate income from your portfolio in order to meet your retirement goals, then you need to take on "enough risk" to generate that income. For example, if you had a $1 million portfolio and needed to generate $40,000 per year from it, but your $1 million portfolio was invested in eight different CDs with a combined yield of 2%, then you would not be generating enough income from the portfolio. The reality in this scenario would be that you would very soon start to dip into principal because you were not generating enough income. And we do not want to dip into principal.

The key to understanding how much "risk" you should be taking on will be driven by the work you do with your Retirement Roadmap. The more income you will need from the portfolio, the more risk you will need to take. If you do not need, now or for the foreseeable future, income from the portfolio, then you can afford to take on very little risk with your money.

Risk is not about losing money. Risk is about understanding how your portfolio needs to be positioned so that you don't run out of money. And if you take "no risk" with your money, depending upon your circumstances and needs in retirement, the real risk you take is running out of money. The big mistake people make when putting together investment portfolios for retirement is not taking on the "proper risk" to meet their retirement needs. This is driven more by the planning than it is by the investment selection.

Without the Retirement Roadmap, you will not truly understand how much "risk" you should be taking.

CHAPTER 2
FUNDAMENTALS OF PLANNING
WHAT YOUR PARENTS NEVER TAUGHT YOU ABOUT INVESTING AND PLANNING FOR RETIREMENT

There is a wonderful poem that was written by Robert Fulghum entitled "All I Really Need To Know I Learned In Kindergarten." I offer it to you below for a refresher course:

All I really need to know about how to live and what to do and how to be I learned in kindergarten. Wisdom was not at the top of the graduate school mountain, but there in the sand pile at school.

These are the things I learned:
- Share everything.
- Play fair.
- Don't hit people.
- Put things back where you found them.
- Clean up your own mess.
- Don't take things that aren't yours.
- Say you're sorry when you hurt somebody.
- Wash your hands before you eat.
- Flush.

- Warm cookies and cold milk are good for you.
- Live a balanced life — learn some and think some and draw and paint and sing and dance and play and work every day some.
- Take a nap every afternoon.
- When you go out in the world, watch out for traffic, hold hands and stick together.
- Be aware of wonder. Remember the little seed in the Styrofoam cup: the roots go down and the plant goes up and nobody really knows how or why, but we are all like that.
- Goldfish and hamsters and white mice and even the little seed in the Styrofoam cup — they all die. So do we.
- And then remember the Dick-and-Jane books and the first word you learned — the biggest word of all — LOOK.

I still love warm cookies and cold milk, I try to share everything (still working on that one) and now the older I get, taking a nap every afternoon has become important again. However, the lessons that we learned in kindergarten about how to lead our lives had little to do with how to plan for retirement. There were no lessons taught in kindergarten through 12th grade — or for that matter, for most of us, in college — about planning for investments, taxes, estate planning or the journey into retirement.

This chapter is dedicated to providing some of the lessons that most of us did not get early on. These lessons are important to learn if we are to maximize the journey into and through retirement.

Investment Lessons

Gaining Proper Perspective

It is not surprising to me that so many people have such a poor grasp on the investment planning process; through the years, we really have been getting mixed signals.

One of the finest mutual fund managers of all time, Peter Lynch, managed Fidelity's Magellan fund. His long-term track record was spectacular and he

> ### INVESTMENT LESSONS
> · Gaining Proper Perspective
> · Having Proper Diversification

was recognized as being tops in his class. When Peter decided to retire, Fidelity named Morris Smith his successor. These were big shoes to fill, and there were many people and organizations who took a keen interest in how Morris would do with the Magellan fund.

A major Boston newspaper decided to track the Magellan fund after Morris Smith started managing it. Every week they would report the performance of the fund. This scorecard may have been good in generating interest in the newspaper, but it was a disservice to those who were trying to learn how to invest properly.

If we are planning for a 30- to 40-year journey through retirement, what happens on a week-to-week basis with any particular investment is, for the most part, irrelevant. The lesson this newspaper was teaching its readers was that it was important to gauge the performance of your investment portfolio weekly. This was absolutely the wrong lesson to be teaching to investors.

One of the things that we have been telling retail investors is to think in an ultra-short-term way, as evidenced by the weekly scorecards and now through the Internet and on many talking-head shows. We showcase the minute-by-minute, hour-by-hour progress of the markets. That is just wrong. And there is another lesson that has been shared by the investment industry with their customers, you and me, and that is the story of *ultra-long-term* investing.

The story goes that as long as we invest in the stock market, we should average somewhere around a 10% per year return. This, they tell us, is the return we should expect based on the past 100 years' performance. Obviously, they tell us, there is no guarantee of future performance. Even at a higher level, and I refer to the institutional managers that I have had the privilege to listen to at many conferences, the message is basically the same. "They" put up colorful charts and graphs indicating that over the past 50 to 70 years the portfolios managed by their institutions have received a certain percentage return. Their message has been to "stay the course."

So the signals are mixed. We have certain organizations telling us that we need to review our portfolios and their performance on a weekly basis, and other organizations telling us to just stay the course. The answer, as is often the case, is somewhere in between.

Part of the frustration that we feel with these volatile and uncertain markets is that we have not been getting the returns we had anticipated, or planned on. And as we grow older and move closer to retirement, we feel more unease about the prospects of a successful retirement and we don't feel like we have a handle on properly investing our money.

I wish I had better news for you, but sometimes a reality

DOW JONES INDUSTRIAL AVERAGE, 1900 TO 2008

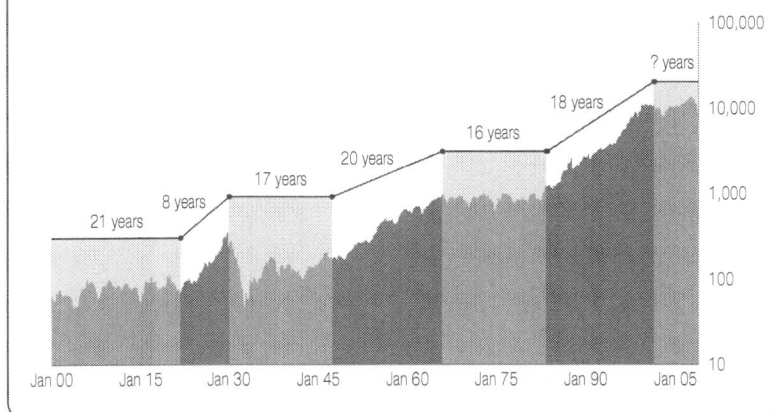

This example is for illustrative purposes only. Performance displayed represents past performance and is no guarantee of future results. The Dow Jones Industrial Average is unmanaged and is unavailable for direct investment. Returns do not reflect any management fees, transaction costs or expenses.
Source: djindexes.com

check is important. So let's take a look at the chart to see if we can get a proper perspective on what to expect looking forward with investments.

The chart is a reflection of what has transpired with the Dow Jones Industrial Average over a period of 108 years. I believe that there are two important lessons to be learned from this chart.

The first lesson deals with expectations. Our industry has told you that you should expect somewhere between a 9% and 10% rate of return over long periods of time. What they did not tell you was that the returns you will experience will be erratic. The chart shows clearly that there have been four protracted secular bear markets. A secular bear market is a market that from point A to point B has no return. However, each year within the bear market you can experience an up

51

or down year.

As you review the chart you will see that there are four periods of flat returns. These periods of flat returns have lasted 21, 17 and 16 years, with the current one, so far, lasting 10 years.

The period that we are in right now is very different than the secular trend that we all experienced in the '80s and '90s where it seemed every time we turned around the market was up another 22%. In the past 108 years we have experienced three secular bull markets, during which the markets performed exceedingly well.

When you look at the chart, you will see that for long periods of time you get no returns, yet for certain periods of time you get extraordinary returns. *If you are within five to seven years from retirement, it is important to give proper consideration to the cycles we are in and plan accordingly.*

The other lesson that we need to learn is to recognize that we *are* in a secular bear market. There are numerous studies that conclude that one must invest differently in a bear market than in a bull market, like the one we enjoyed in the '80s and '90s.

The phrase "buy and hold" was one that we seemed to be familiar with. We were told to buy quality, stay the course and the market would reward us. Studies indicate, however, that the buy-and-hold philosophy has less of a probability of outperforming a "flat" market than does a more nimble and alternative-driven portfolio.

In markets such as the one we are experiencing now, the managers able to be more nimble and to make more frequent allocation adjustments to their portfolios are the managers of choice. These managers are more tactical than strategic, and many of them can both long and short the markets. Fortunately, in the past few years more of these institutional managers have become available to the retail investor (previously they were only available to those with at least $5 million to $15 million to invest).

Alternative investments are investments that are designed to complement a "core" portfolio. A core portfolio would hold traditional stocks, bonds and cash. The alternative investments should have a low correlation to the core portfolio. This low correlation should mean that these alternative investments would move in directions that would not be tied to traditional market directions. These investments could move up or down regardless of the traditional markets' movements.

Alternative investment categories could include investments in currencies, commodities, managed futures, long/short funds, arbitrage funds, unlisted REITs, natural resources and more. Again, over the past few years more of these investment vehicles have become available to the retail investor.

There is no guarantee for any future performance, regardless of the type of approach that you take. However, it does appear that we may be in for another three to five years of "flat" performance, and the use of more nimble and alternative-driven portfolios should replace the old "buy and hold" portfolios.

Having Proper Diversification

Having eight certificates of deposit in different banks, or eight different large-cap growth mutual funds, is not proper diversification. Traditionally, diversification meant that we could have stocks and bonds in different sectors and by being in different sectors could moderate our returns. The theory went that as one sector would go up the other would go down, and we could avoid having such volatile swings in our portfolios. We learned a very difficult lesson in 2008, when basically all sectors dropped precipitously with no safety net in sight.

By utilizing more tactical managers and bringing in more alternative investments, you bring even more diversification to your portfolio. With this approach you could take out some of the volatility that we are so afraid of, yet potentially still achieve an attractive return. (Certainly there are no guarantees for future performance.)

Back in the '80s and '90s there were very popular charts that indicated if you missed the top 10 days of a market, the long-term performance of your overall portfolio would suffer greatly. The studies have now been expanded and instead of just focusing on the top 10 days, the new studies also take into account what would happen if you missed the 10 worst days. And the conclusions are startling.

If you missed the best performance days, your returns decreased by approximately two-thirds. However, your returns more than tripled if you missed the *worst* performance days. So as much as we wish to participate in the up days, it is even more important to avoid the down days. By incorporating more tactical and alternative investing, you bring in investment vehicles that may be better suited to help buffer the portfolio from the really bad days.

So I believe the most important lesson one can learn with your investments during these difficult times is to recognize

IMPACT OF THE TEN BEST AND WORST DAYS

Days	Growth of $1	Cumulative Return (%)
Capture 10 best and worst	58.73	5,704
Miss 10 best	19.25	1,825
Miss 10 worst	184.30	18,330
Miss 10 best and worst	61.13	6,013

Source: Bloomberg L.P.

what cycle we are in and make sure that the investments you own reflect the type of investing climate that we are in.

Planning Lessons

Creating Retirement Goals

I believe one of the biggest mistakes people make is not coordinating all of their goals properly, which begs the question of actually having goals. It is one thing to say that you would like to retire and you would like to get a certain amount of return on your portfolio, but without truly understanding the details and without setting clear and definable goals, the probability of your accomplishing/maximizing the journey into retirement could be compromised.

If I had a nickel for every time someone came up to me and asked me if "this mutual fund" or "this stock" was a good investment, I would be a very rich man. The answer I gave was the same every time: "Without understanding what your retirement goals are, or what risk you are willing to take with your portfolio, or the risk you *should* take with your portfolio, I cannot give an intelligent answer."

PLANNING LESSONS

· Creating Retirement Goals
· Reducing the Impact of Taxes
· The Benefits of Coordination
· Dealing with our Emotions
· Understanding the Transition into Retirement
· Redefining Your Objectives

Experts tell us to analyze and understand what we invest in, but you have not been told how important it is to sync up your retirement goals with your investments. And without understanding *exactly* what your retirement needs are, how can we possibly understand how good or bad a particular investment is relative to your overall goals? This is why a Retirement Roadmap is so crucial to the foundation of helping you to pursue the retirement of your dreams.

I believe there is a great misunderstanding about the concept of investment risk within an investor's portfolio. Too many people believe that you can only take so much risk, and they would prefer to be risk averse. The reality is you could also take on too little risk, which could mean that you would not be able to achieve the retirement lifestyle you desire.

So the question isn't "Is this investment good?" The correct question should be "Is the risk that I am taking with this investment suitable given my retirement goal?" For the answer to taking on the proper amount of risk can only be found once you understand how much income you need in retirement.

The lesson to be learned here is that you need to sync up your retirement goals with your investment portfolio in order to make sure that you are taking on the "proper" risk.

What is interesting, when we coordinate all of the moving parts for the Retirement Roadmap, is that you can actually get a handle on certain areas that you could not previously. One of those areas is taxes.

If I could show you a way to reduce your taxes, would you be interested? Of course you would.

So let's take a look at two scenarios and see how the planning for each is different. The setting of this will be a couple about to retire, both 66 years old, with a $500,000 investment portfolio. Of the $500,000, $300,000 is in an IRA rollover and $200,000 is in a taxable, jointly owned investment account.

For the first scenario, the couple has a retirement income need of $70,000 and between pensions and Social Security checks they are receiving $70,000. So they have no need to generate income from their investment portfolio.

For the second scenario, the couple has a retirement income need of $70,000 but is only receiving $60,000 between their pensions and Social Security checks. So they have a need to generate income of $10,000 from their portfolios.

Let's assume that in each scenario, the couple wants to invest in traditional stocks and bonds. Let us also assume they wish to take on the proper amount of risk and that they have already set aside the proper emergency reserves; therefore they can fully invest in the two investment buckets we just identified. We can also assume that they would prefer not to dip into principal if at all possible. Typically, there is more income generated with a bond or bond fund than there is in a stock or stock fund, and the couple is comfortable with both. For these hypothetical situations I will assume that the bond portfolio can generate a 4% yield and the stock portfolio a 1% yield.

For the first scenario, the couple has decided they would like to take on prudent investment risk. Even though they don't need income from the portfolio they still need to overcome the impact of inflation, and would like to take some trips and make some major purchases in the future. Therefore they have decided to invest in a portfolio that has a 50% allocation to bonds and 50% to stocks.

So the real question here, since we do not need to generate an income, is how to minimize the impact of taxes on the earnings and capital gains. The key to minimizing tax exposure is not in the actual selection of the investments, but in how they are held.

Assuming that the majority of the total return for a bond or bond fund is in the yield, then in order to reduce the impact of taxes on the yield it would be better for them to hold the majority of the bond portfolio inside their IRA. If they were to hold the bonds in the taxable account, all of the yield would be exposed to taxes — assuming they are taxable bonds. By owning these investments properly (inside the IRA), they would be paying less in taxes.

Assuming that the majority of the total return for a stock or stock fund is with the capital appreciation potential, it would be proper to own the majority of the stock portfolio in the taxable account. Typically you would owe little or no tax on a stock or stock mutual fund unless you realized capital appreciation. Therefore if all you did was just to hold the stock or stock fund, then you could minimize the impact of taxes because you would have little in the way of realized capital gains.

Thus, in order to reduce the impact of taxes, the couple in scenario one is better off to hold the majority of the bond allocation inside the IRA and the majority of the stock allocation to the taxable account.

For the couple in the second scenario, the issue is different. Here, this couple needs to generate income from the portfolio. *So the big question here is how do I generate the income I need in a tax-efficient manner, and which account should it come from?* Understanding how to answer this question will not only help us to properly coordinate the investment portfolio with our retirement goals, but also give us the opportunity to minimize tax exposure.

In this scenario, we should own the bond portfolio in the jointly held taxable account and the stocks in the IRA (the opposite of the first scenario). We would generate a 4% yield on $200,000 (the jointly held account), which would account for an additional $8000 of income. This income would be taxed at favorable rates because this is dividend income. We would then need to make a distribution from the IRA of only $2000, where this distribution would be considered ordinary income.

So not only is it important to recognize what investments to own and how to coordinate them with your retirement goals, but also to understand what part of the investment journey you are on and how to own each investment properly in order to minimize your tax exposure.

To reiterate, when discussing financial planning there is too much emphasis on investment selection. The real work within the world of financial planning, and particularly the transitioning into retirement, is in the development of the Retirement Roadmap. It is more important to know what your income need is, and to own the investments in the right accounts, than it is to own the right investments.

If you do the work properly and understand the nuances of the distribution phase, then you can put yourself in a position to reduce your tax exposure.

The Benefits of Coordination

In order to make my point about the importance of coordinating your financial affairs, I would like to share with you a story. This is a story of a couple who are both in their late 50s and have two children going to college. It is not unusual for me to see people in this situation, as it seems that we are having children a little later in life and college-funding issues become a retirement planning problem. From a planning perspective it can be very difficult to attempt to take care of both college and retirement planning at the same time.

This couple was wrestling with a number of issues simultaneously. First, the overriding issue was that he was hoping to retire within the next three to five years, but the market was not cooperating and he was no longer sure that he would be able to. He had lost a lot of money in the market and a lot of faith in his financial advisor. Second, they were tapping into their retirement nest egg to pay for the college expenses. They were beginning to understand that if they continued along this path, they could potentially bankrupt their retirement by putting their kids through college. Third, they were unsure about how much life insurance they should own and how to pay for it. Fourth, they were getting bombarded with literature with regard to long-term care insurance because they were now on everybody's list. Finally, the most daunting task facing them was that they had two different brokers, two different insurance agents, an accountant and several friends all providing "guidance." They were totally confused and unsure of how to move forward with addressing the issues ahead of them.

The first thing that we did for them was to put in place the foundation for the Retirement Roadmap. We went back to basics: What were their goals, what was important to them, and how would they like to prioritize all of the issues facing them? Once we spent some time developing their roadmap, the solutions became much clearer for them.

Next, we put in place the proper portfolio for him. Because he had lost faith and trust in the person who was giving him financial advice, his broker, he had taken over control of the investment portfolio without really knowing what to do.

Third, we addressed the issue of how to pay for the college expenses. They were fortunate to have enough equity in the house, and agreed it was better to pay a portion of the college expenses through the tax-deductible expense of a mortgage. They were also given guidance as to how to go back to their children to explain to them that the financial situation had changed dramatically and there had to be a reality check for all involved. The kids stepped up to the plate and agreed to take on a portion of the college expenses by taking out some college loans.

Fourth, they did not have enough life insurance. The best-laid plans will blow up if the unintended happens and you are not prepared. This is why we buy insurance. We helped guide them in better understanding how to put together a properly programmed life insurance portfolio and directed them to go back to the life insurance agent to purchase the correct amount of insurance.

Fifth, we addressed the issue of long-term care insurance. Many years ago there were all sorts of estate planning strategies available to protect one's assets in the event of a long-term care situation. For most of middle-class America, there are now very few of these strategies left. Long-term care insurance can be an excellent solution in the right scenario. For this couple, long-term care insurance was suitable. However, the timing wasn't right. So we agreed to put long-term care insurance programming on the back burner and evaluate it again in 3 to 4 years when the kids were out of college. Cash flow was too tight, with two kids in college, to add the cost of long-term care insurance to their budget.

Finally, they needed a "go to" trusted financial advisor who could coordinate all of the issues and be the quarterback in an effort to find the correct solutions for them. This couple had too many voices saying too many different things, creating a tremendous amount of confusion and anxiety. When they chose to work with us, they were able to clearly and concisely understand what they needed to do and how to get there. *Simplifying the decision-making process helped them to get back on track toward pursuing a successful retirement.*

Dealing with our Emotions

I want to spend a few moments addressing the issue of how emotions play into our decision-making process. I have always said that the role of a financial planner is 50% psychiatrist and 50% planner, and in order to be successful you have to play both roles successfully.

Many years ago a client came to me with a series of concerns which we discussed for over an hour, and as she left she told me my new title should be "Dr. Feel Good." Obviously, I was very glad that she felt good after spending the hour with me but it was important to understand, from my perspective, what it really meant when she used the phrase "Dr. Feel Good."

An easy way, and the path of least resistance, would have been just to paint rosy pictures for her when addressing her concerns, so that she "felt good" about the meeting. But that is not what happened. We addressed head-on the series of issues that were causing her great concern. We separated the "facts" from the "emotions" in order to get a clear picture of the issues.

It is important to recognize that we all come with a certain perspective, and we react to certain scenarios differently. It is often the case that when two people look at the same set of "facts," they "see" things differently. It is the way that we filter "how" we see things that brings a unique and personal perspective to how we make decisions. Many times we are unable to separate the facts that we "see" from the "reality" that is in front of us. It is at these times that *emotions* drive our decision-making process, and that is often not a good thing.

Often it is about bringing proper perspective to how we see things, and with this perspective we can then make intelligent decisions. As "Dr. Feel Good" it was not about just feeding her answers that felt good — it was about bringing proper perspective to the decision-making process and feeling good about those decisions.

I feel that one of the most important lessons that can be learned is that what we "see" may be different than what is actually in front of us. When we understand this dynamic, and take a little bit of extra time to work through the issues, then we will make better decisions that are more in line with what our overall objectives are.

Understanding the Transition into Retirement

I believe that one of the biggest mistakes people make when it comes to retirement is a lack of understanding of the transition process into this next stage of life. One of the most valuable lessons one can learn when it comes to planning for retirement is the necessity to *prepare* for this new chapter. There are many studies which indicate that those who are truly successful in retirement are those who have taken the time to understand how to *fill the time* in their daily lives which used to be concerned with "work."

The concept of working, or to put it another way, no longer working, is more than just about the paycheck. The workplace fills many needs that we have — including, but not limited to a reason to get out of bed, a social network, a sense of accomplishment, a feeling of self-esteem and much more. Certainly when you retire you have to replace the "paycheck;" however, that is not all you have to replace.

Those who have a place to go to, a hobby or passion to pursue, will have the best probability of having a "successful" journey into retirement. The 40, 50 or 60 hours a week that you earmarked for work can now be replaced by important tasks that could include the pursuit of a second or third career, volunteer activities, grand-parenting duties, more rounds of golf and much more. The people that I talk to who feel they have "successfully" retired are those people who make the following statement — "I don't know how I had the time to go to work before, I have so much to do now."

Take the time to sit down alone, or with your spouse or family, to determine how you're going to spend your time in retirement. Think of it as opening up an entirely new business and needing to plan for its success. You cannot just hang a shingle outside the door, sit behind the desk, and hope you will be a successful business person. You will need to put down the proper business plan and allow for the flexibility to make the changes necessary so that you can fully enjoy your journey into, and through, retirement.

You can find a questionnaire to help you with this on our website (see introduction for details).

Redefining Your Objectives

One of the items necessary to address when you are planning for your transition into retirement is a reevaluation of your objectives. When you are working, your objectives are that you wish to accumulate as much money as possible in order to have a successful retirement. When you engage the process of putting together your Retirement Roadmap, that objective may change.

We have already addressed the issue of syncing up your money management with your retirement objectives, and that concept holds true as you start defining what retirement will be for you and your family. Let me share with you a story of a client that will help you better understand exactly what I mean.

John and Dolores, both in their mid-60s, were about to retire. They had spent their working years taking care of their family and attempting to accumulate as much money as possible to enjoy the retirement they so richly deserved. During their working years, they paid great attention to how they were investing their money and took on what they thought was a prudent amount of risk in order to accumulate the nest egg they had developed. However, they were not sure how much risk to take now that they were headed into retirement.

One of the common misconceptions is that as you retire, so does your money. The reality is that even though you may retire, you still must manage your money prudently over the next 25 to 35 years in order to make sure you can do what you want to do, when you want to do it. Just sticking the money under the mattress in order to preserve its value, and not taking on "risk" because you are afraid your nest egg will be depleted if there is a correction in the market, is not the correct way to approach money management during your retirement years. When we worked with John and Dolores to initiate their Retirement Roadmap, we needed to understand how to properly invest their accumulated nest egg now that they were about to retire. Fortunately for them, the cash flow that they needed in order to pursue their successful retirement was covered by their pension and Social Security income — there was no need to generate any income from the portfolio. As a matter of fact, because their desire was to live a simple life, they would not need income from the portfolio for many years to come, if ever.

As a result of the planning process, John and Dolores recognized that their objective for money management had changed dramatically. It was no longer about accumulating assets; it was about preserving and protecting them during their retirement years, and beyond. We decided to take a conservative approach with their money, which was different than the growth-oriented portfolio they had managed during their working years. This did not mean we just put the money in the bank or under the mattress — it meant being cautious.

The management of the money for John and Dolores would have been very different if they needed to generate income from the portfolio in order to pursue their retirement lifestyle. If they needed income from the portfolio, we would have taken on a more growth-oriented approach, but for them it was not necessary. By doing the Retirement Roadmap for them, we took the mystery out of the decision-making process and they now knew *exactly* what they needed to do in order to manage their money properly, keeping in mind their new objectives.

The Two Stages of Financial Planning

There are two distinct phases when it comes to financial planning and your retirement — the first is the accumulation stage, and the second is the distribution stage. The accumulation stage refers to those years while you are working, when you are hoping to put away as much money as possible for your retirement. The distribution phase is when you are looking to convert those accumulated assets into income or liquidity needed to pursue your successful retirement. The planning for these two distinct stages can be very different, and different planning strategies need to be employed.

This gets back to the study I referenced earlier from a noted mutual fund company, which indicated that during your working years you engaged 2½ financial advisors, yet as you approach retirement you are looking for one "go to" retirement planning specialist. I bring this up again because as we discuss how you transition into retirement, this may mean transitioning your "team" of advisers. Certainly you would want people who specialize in your stage of financial planning in order to maximize the value of the advice that you're getting. This is where a specialist may be more appropriate for your "team" than a generalist.

The conversations that you will have with your team of advisers now will be different than the conversations you had during your working years. I have found that these conversations have been taken to a higher level and often demand new strategies be taken. Instead of just focusing on the money management aspect of financial planning, we now spend time talking about estate planning, tax-efficient distribution of income, gifting or charitable bequests, preservation and protection of assets, and much more. It is the *coordination* of all of these various aspects of financial planning that makes the world of retirement planning much more complex.

The lesson here is that you need to align yourself with the appropriate set of advisers who can help you accomplish your new set of objectives as you transition into retirement.

Taking the Mystery Out

One of my favorite stories is about a client who called me to find out if she could replace her kitchen cabinets. Clearly, she was not asking me for advice on building the kitchen cabinets, because I am the furthest thing from a handyman. What she was asking in this simple question was really a series of questions: Do I have the money to buy new kitchen cabinets? If I do, where does the money come from? If I take the money, will it impact my current income? And most importantly, if I spend the money *today* on the kitchen cabinets, will I have the money I need *tomorrow*?

In my practice I have called this the "kitchen cabinet" question, and it comes in many forms: Can I take the trip? Can I buy another car? Can I earmark money to fund college expenses for my grandchild? Can I buy a second home? These are just some of the questions that address the concern "if I spend my money *today* will it be there *tomorrow*?" Without the benefit of a clearly defined Retirement Roadmap, the answer to the question is not always easily understood.

The true benefit of having done the proper planning is that when something new comes up you can go back to the plan, and determine what would happen if you changed some of the assumptions based on the new objectives, to see if your roadmap still works. The beauty is that you can see the result before you make the decision — to buy the car, to do the kitchen cabinets, to go on that trip.

Without a properly defined roadmap, you may never truly know whether or not the decisions you are about to make will impact your ability to continue to pursue your retirement dreams. Furthermore, your decisions could be constantly second-guessed, which would mean you would never truly gain a sense of peace of mind.

Asset Preservation Lessons

When you have accumulated the assets necessary to retire,

the conversations go to a different level. The truth is that there are *three big questions* when it comes to the financial planning for my clients: First, am I sure that the assets that are available to me and my spouse will generate the income needed during our retirement? Second, when I am gone will my spouse be taken care of? And third, when we are both gone will we have put together the necessary planning to take care of the children and grandchildren?

The area I think is important to address at this stage of the conversation is *insurance programming*. My goal here is to make you aware of how to think about some of the tools and strategies available to you. There are plenty of books and resources that go into great detail explaining how to actually put in place the proper planning; my objective is just to bring your awareness to a higher level.

Let's start with the issue of life insurance. When it comes to life insurance, as it relates to your retirement planning, I believe there are two profiles where life insurance is important.

The First Profile

If one or the other of a couple were to die tomorrow, and as a result of that death an income stream would be lost, then life insurance would be an appropriate solution. If, for example, you were receiving a $50,000 pension and were to pass away, and that pension did not provide a survivor's benefit, then having a life insurance policy that could replace that $50,000 of lost income would be a strategy worth pursuing.

One of the planning strategies available, marrying the concepts of pensions and life insurance, is what we call the *Pension Maximization Strategy*.

Typically, you are offered three or four options for your pension. One of those options is to take the full benefit today, with no survivorship available. So when you pass, there is nothing available for your surviving spouse. Or, you could take the 100% option, which would mean you would take a lesser share than the full share available today, so that when you pass your spouse would continue to receive the pension you had been receiving, in full. There are also options in between the 0% survivorship and the 100% survivorship options.

So what are the risks of taking one pension option versus another? Let us assume you wish to take care of your surviving spouse upon your passing; therefore, take the 100% survivorship option. However, if your spouse predeceases you, you will be left with the wrong pension.

Why do I say the wrong pension? Because you chose, with your irrevocable decision, to take a lower pension so that you could provide 100% of that pension to your surviving spouse. But in this scenario, your surviving spouse passed first. This leaves you with a pension which is less than what you could have if you had chosen the zero survivorship option, because you are paying a premium to provide a benefit to a spouse.

Let's look at an example: You are about to retire and you are offered, based on your and your spouse's respective ages, a pension of $80,000. If you were to take the 0% survivorship option you could receive the full $80,000 today, and for as long as you live. Once you pass, your spouse is no longer eligible for any pension. You may also have the ability to take a 100% survivorship option, which would mean you could take a $60,000 per year pension for as long as you, *and* your spouse, live.

Getting back to the risk of taking the 100% survivorship option, if your spouse passes first then you will be giving up $20,000 per year of income; that was, in essence, the premium for having a survivorship pension available. So what is the solution?

The Pension Maximization Strategy is a hybrid of the 0% and the 100% pension options offered by your company. However, it is not a formal option available through your company. By going back to the Retirement Roadmap you can determine, in advance, the impact of either one of you dying first. Based on the information in the Retirement Roadmap, it may be determined that you can minimize your risk by utilizing the Pension Maximization Strategy.

This strategy marries the purchase of a life insurance policy with the 0% survivorship option so that neither you nor your spouse will be without the appropriate income. In essence, it takes the risk out of who will die first. You see, the pension options are based on actuarial experiences. We do not know when we select the pension option who will survive whom. *By utilizing the Pension Maximization Strategy you maximize the value of the money available to you, and your spouse, for your retirement.*

The Second Profile

If your estate is large enough that it will incur an estate death tax, either on the federal or state level, then owning life insurance is a strategy that should be considered — if your estate planning objective is to pass your estate on *completely* to your heirs.

Getting back to the planning, and your planning objectives, it is important to understand what you wish to do with your estate once you are gone. Most people would prefer to avoid the impact of estate death taxes on their estate, because it means that money would be coming out of the estate rather than going to the designated beneficiaries. If this is how you think about estate planning, then owning the proper type of life insurance within an irrevocable life insurance trust is a strategy that should be discussed with your financial planner and your estate planning attorney.

An important lesson to learn about life insurance is that for many people the wrong amount of insurance is owned. I find that people are not as aware as they should be when it comes to the options with regard to pensions, but are also unaware what to do with existing life insurance policies that continue to require annual premium payments.

One of the fun stories I can share with you is of a client who did a Retirement Roadmap with us and, as a result, found out she did not need two of the small life insurance policies that she currently owned. We helped guide her through the conversations with her insurance agent to determine if there was a cash surrender available if she were to surrender the policy.

She surrendered the two insurance policies, received checks in the amount of $8000, and with the proceeds took her two children to Hawaii and enjoyed the vacation of a lifetime. Without the Retirement Roadmap, without understanding the true purpose or nature of the existing life insurance policies, we would never have been able to come to the conclusion that these policies were not necessary, nor create the opportunity for a wonderful trip full of a lifetime of memories.

Long-Term Care Insurance

Another strategy to help preserve assets is the purchase of long-term care insurance. As more and more of the options that used to be available within the world of Medicaid planning are no longer available, long-term care insurance has become a sound piece of an asset protection strategy.

Again, there are many books and resources available with regard to what to purchase when considering a long-term care insurance policy. My intent here is to raise your awareness with regard to how to *think* about long-term care insurance. Many of the people that I speak with are already on those "lists" for marketing purposes, and they are getting inundated with information and requests to purchase long-term care insurance.

A common objection to long-term care insurance is the price. The Retirement Roadmap, again, can provide the answer as to whether or not you can *afford* a long-term care insurance program. *The question really does become, if I pay long-term care insurance annual premiums, how will it impact my cash flow today, and tomorrow?*

I often counsel my clients to pay the annual premium out of one of their investments. Instead of having it come out of "cash flow," have the annual premium taken from one of the investment line items that is earmarked annually to be the source for payment for the insurance.

By going back to the Retirement Roadmap and plugging in the annual premiums, you can easily determine, beforehand, whether or not long-term care insurance is for you.

CHAPTER 3
WHAT THE FUTURE HOLDS

HOW TO GET WHERE YOU WANT TO GO WITH PROPER PLANNING

When my daughter signed the rental agreement for her very first apartment, she was so excited that she wanted to share her joy with me. We agreed to meet for lunch at the mall, which she told me was just a couple of minutes away from her apartment, and then go over to see her new place.

After lunch, I followed her in my car and soon realized she did not know where to go. We seemed to be driving in a big circle.

Using my navigation system I punched in her address, and the route we were looking for was displayed. I called her on my cell phone and told her to follow me.

The two-minute drive took us almost 15 minutes, because we didn't know exactly how to get from the mall (point A) to the apartment (point B). When we finally got to the apartment, we agreed that next time she should probably have a better set of directions. We both had a good laugh.

If you recall the Alice in Wonderland story, my daughter and I were bound to get somewhere if only we drove long enough. This scenario plays out over and over again within the world of retirement planning. You know where you are, you know where you want to end up, but without an efficient roadmap to help you get from point A to point B it may be a while before you get to your final destination, if ever.

In this chapter, you will gain some insight as to what the benefits of proper planning can do for you and your retirement.

In Chapter 2, in the section called Asset Preservation Lessons, I listed three big questions that are often brought up by my clients when dealing with the issue of transitioning into and through retirement. These questions serve as the foundation for almost all of the issues when developing their roadmap. If we are to provide peace of mind for our clients, then we need to deal head-on with the issues of the day and make sure they are able to sleep well at night.

The Bucket List

You may recall the movie starring Jack Nicholson and Morgan Freeman that chronicled two people who had been given a short time to live, and their pursuit of checking off all of the items on their Bucket List.

One of the very important questions I ask my clients is "What would you do if money were not the issue; how would you lead your life?" It is a very difficult question to answer honestly for most people — we're so inclined to be cautious about how we spend money that we don't let ourselves dream BIG. So instead of saying "I'd like to take a six-week cruise," we will say "one-week excursion." Instead of taking the grandkids away every year during spring school break, we take them once to Disney World, and instead of upgrading that 50-year-old kitchen, we buy another set of drapes in an effort to bring new life to the room.

These are just a few examples of some of the issues that I have talked about with clients where they have not allowed themselves to think big, because they were too concerned about the impact of spending money today and how they could live tomorrow.

I submit that one of the more fun exercises that you can do with your spouse and family is to develop a Bucket List unencumbered by what you think you can do. Let your mind go wild and put down, in no particular order, bold plans to do things that you just didn't think were possible. Then go back to your Retirement Roadmap and put in the costs and time needed to accomplish these goals.

You can find a worksheet to develop your own bucket list on our website (see introduction for details).

It is important, when pursuing this exercise, to be as specific and precise as possible. Instead of just putting down "a trip to Europe," put down "go to Italy for two weeks next August that will cost about $20,000." If you only put down that you would like to go to Europe, you never quantify exactly how much it will cost, nor are you able to visualize the length of stay or the places you will visit. The more you can actually quantify the items on your Bucket List, the more measurable it will be when you go back to your Retirement Roadmap to find out whether or not you can accomplish your goals.

The roadmap, then, will indicate what you need to do in

order to accomplish your BIG goals. It may be that you can actually do everything you wished to on your Bucket List, and you just never knew that. Or you may be able to accomplish a portion of the Bucket List, which is more than you would have done before — because you had no Bucket List.

I talk to many people who are anxious about spending money today. To me, the real shame of not coordinating your Bucket List with your Retirement Roadmap is that you may be able to accomplish some of those very important items on your Bucket List but choose not to, out of fear.

Cash Is King

The key to a successful retirement is cash flow. One definition of a successful retirement is to do what you want to do when you want to do it. Regardless of how much you are worth, if you don't have enough cash flow then you will not have a successful retirement. However, it goes beyond just having the cash; it is how to utilize the cash flow in an efficient manner.

Without understanding your cash flow needs, it will be very difficult to establish the correct investment portfolio for your situation, take on the proper amount of risk, create tax-efficient income, potentially reduce the impact of both income and estate death taxes, and so much more.

How will you know if gifting $20,000 to your grandchild's college education fund will impact your cash flow need at a later date? How will you determine the impact of buying a second home? How will you know if it is all right to spend $30,000 on the cruise of a lifetime?

All of this can be easily understood once you input what you wish to accomplish during your retirement years to the Retirement Roadmap. With proper planning, you can take the mystery out of the decision-making process. Let me share with you a couple of stories from my 25 years of experience in dealing with people who wish to plan for a successful retirement.

If You Could Retire Today, Would You?

Many years ago, I was asked to participate in the *Boston Herald's* money makeover column. The story of one of the couples that I wrote about has become one of the most enduring and powerful stories that I tell at speaking engagements in the Boston area.

During the first phone interview, my objective was to get as much information as possible regarding their goals and objectives for retirement. In the 60-minute interview it became clear that there was one issue more important than any other: She was looking forward to retiring in five years (at age 65).

Although she did not enjoy her job, in her view, 65 was the "magical" year to retire because that is when she was going to maximize her pension. As we probed deeper, it became clear that she was really dreading working for the next five years. She felt the job was taking a toll on her physically, but she was committed to maximizing the pension.

After the initial interview, they sent me a packet of relevant financial data. This package included the specifics of their retirement assets and investments, a copy of their recent taxes, a cash flow worksheet and an initial draft of their Bucket List.

During the next interview I asked many questions regarding the information they had sent. How had they put together the investment portfolio? What kind of risk were they willing to take with their money? And as is typical when I ask these two particular questions, they were not really sure why they had the type of investments that they had or what their real risk tolerance was.

You can find an example of a cash flow worksheet on our website (see introduction for details).

We then looked at the cash flow worksheet to make sure that the needed cash flow was actually a "real" need. Often, when we review these cash flow worksheets, updates are needed. Most people have a difficult time assessing their actual need, and it is only once we review line item by line item do we get a number that is more accurate.

One of the most common mistakes I find when doing a cash flow evaluation is that most people forget a very important line item — the one pertaining to taxes.

So when someone comes to me stating they need $7000 a month of income, they are typically referring to only the money they spend, not the amount that needs to be generated in income. The reality for someone who needs to spend $7000 a month is that they have to account for the impact of income taxes, so the true need may actually be almost $9000 a month. Based on the information I received, I drafted the initial Retirement Roadmap for them in preparation for our final call. My objective was to come up with recommendations that would be suitable for their situation.

I started that call with a question: "If you could retire today, would you?" The answer she gave me was the one I expected — she felt that she had to work until she was 65 in order to maximize her pension income. It was at this point that I had to re-educate her as to what the proper definition of "retirement" was. By bringing a new definition of retirement to her, I knew that I could change her perspective and the way she was thinking about her own retirement.

Her definition of retirement was to "maximize her pension income." The reality was that if she was able to generate enough cash flow to meet her retirement cash flow need, she could retire whenever she wanted to. It was not about staying on the job long enough to get the pension; it was about how she would live her life through the journey of retirement.

I then shared with her the results of the initial draft of the Retirement Roadmap, which indicated that if she were to retire tomorrow she would have enough income to satisfy her cash flow needs. For her, it was a revelation.

With this newfound perspective, she made a paradigm shift in her thoughts about retiring. She gave her notice three months later and was able to start enjoying life sooner than she thought she could.

What is interesting about this scenario is that this couple was not a "wealthy" couple by traditional standards. They did not have "lots" of money. They simply wanted to enjoy life and be able to do what they wanted to do without feeling stressed.

Without having done the money makeover, she would have worked another five years, hating every day of that job, in order to accomplish what she thought was the proper definition of retirement, which was maximizing that pension. By stepping back and reevaluating the planning, we were able to provide her with a whole new perspective on what retirement could be, and that changed her life for the better.

Uncertainty Breeds Frustration and a Sense of Despair

It seems that I have been having conversations with more people who are experiencing high frustration levels — higher than they have felt in quite some time. What happens is that as we get older and move closer to retirement, or have already transitioned into retirement, a sense of urgency seems to set in. In great part, this is driven by the secular bear market that we are experiencing and its perceived impact on our retirement goals.

The next story is about a couple who felt that they were no longer on track to accomplish their retirement dreams and how it impacted the way they were leading their lives.

Al and Betty are in their early 60s. Al retired from IBM five years ago, while Betty still held onto her 30-hour per week job. They have two boys who are now 16 and 18. In preparation for Al's transition into retirement, we had established a Retirement Roadmap seven years ago. The goal was to be able to send the kids to college without impacting the ability for Al and Betty to enjoy their retirement. At that time, we had earmarked a college annual expense of $20,000 and had assumed that the market would provide us with a reasonable return.

With the eldest boy now applying for college, reality, along with a heightened sense of frustration, was setting in. The market had not provided us with reasonable returns, the $20,000 annual college expense was closer to $30,000 for the colleges they were looking at, and Al and Betty were quite concerned.

Currently Al has a part-time job that complements the pension he is getting as a retiree. He had hoped to stop working completely by now, but is concerned that if he loses that part-time income, their finances will be strained and their retirement compromised.

During one of our semiannual reviews he vented his frustrations about the market performance and was quite upset. Not upset about the market per se — but about its impact on their future retirement lifestyle. We agreed to meet again in one week to go back to the Retirement Roadmap to see where they actually stood.

At the next meeting we updated many of the original assumptions. We took a look at the income that was coming in now, and the projected college outflow over the next six years, and made another adjustment to the return assumptions for the markets over the next five years and beyond. And once we stepped back to reevaluate where we were on the roadmap, things were not as dire as they had feared.

What was truly interesting about this particular meeting was that we started to pick apart some of the other aspects of the planning. One of the assumptions made was that Al would work for another five years in his part-time job. He mentioned he was getting a little weary of working and was wondering when he would be able to stop without impacting their retirement. For Al, it was actually determined that he would only have to work for another two years and that he could have the choice at that time as to whether or not he wanted to continue working. Betty, on the other hand, enjoyed her part-time job, and was looking forward to working for another five years.

Al and Betty's demeanor changed dramatically upon the completion of that meeting. No longer were they feeling a sense of panic as a result of the lack of performance in the markets; instead, they were feeling comfortable that they were still on track to accomplish their retirement goals.

By going back to their roadmap, we were able to take down their frustration levels and empower them to know that they were still headed in the right direction.

The Gift of Freedom

Another example of how powerful the Retirement Roadmap can be is illustrated in the next story. Too often we focus on the markets and how they might impact our ability to retire. However, what truly drives a sense of peace of mind is how we actually "live the journey."

Feeling good about what we do, and making good decisions about how we interact with our families, are very important, often more than the money issues.

Our long-term clients, Harry and Louise, came to us to revisit their plan because a new situation had arisen. We know that things will change, people's priorities change and this situation was no different. Although this couple had a well-working retirement plan, their priorities had shifted a bit.

Louise was now considering leaving the workforce to take care of their 13-year-old daughter. They were worried about her, as she was entering middle school. She would be coming home and staying alone without supervision every day from 2–5 p. m. Louise really wanted to be there for her, but the couple didn't want to sacrifice their retirement. In their 50s, they had made plans to retire in about 8 years.

We reviewed their Retirement Roadmap to reevaluate the numbers if Louise was to now stay home. As we went through their cash flow chart in detail, we found that their current cash flow would be okay if she left the work force, but only if Harry cut his retirement contributions in half.

The good news was that we could solve their immediate cash flow issues. However, Harry expressed concern because he didn't want the reduced contributions to prevent them from meeting their retirement goals. He had always been told to maximize his retirement savings.

We went through the numbers in detail, using the reduced contribution amount but still targeting the same date for retirement. We found that by making some adjustments in the portfolio allocation and rethinking some of our original calculations, the couple could give up Louise's income and have her stay home with their daughter while still being on track to a successful retirement.

Without a Retirement Roadmap, they would not have been able to coordinate the different issues that were concerning them. With proper planning, we took the guesswork out of what they should do and how it would impact them, and gave them the gift of freedom to choose what they wanted. Now they can take care of their family, and their future, feeling confident in their decisions.

Taking Retirement Planning to the Next Level

So far we have addressed retirement planning in fairly traditional terms. We have addressed the issues of money management, tax planning, retirement income, estate planning, insurance programming and much more. And I have chronicled several examples of how important it is to coordinate the various planning issues into your own roadmap in order to help you take the mystery out of some of the decisions that you are faced with.

However, there still is one more step that most people fail to do in order to get retirement planning to the next level.

Many studies indicate that one of the biggest concerns for those facing retirement is the issue of "coordination." Two years ago, my firm organized a focus group for some of our select clients. The objective was to determine whether we were all on the same page in delivering the proper solutions. We chose a Tuesday in February to hold this dinner event. One of the more extraordinary lessons learned that evening actually had nothing to do with the event itself, but the weather. There was a horrific snowstorm that day, and we were concerned about our ability to pull off the event, and about the safety of our clients. As it turned out, all of the clients who had agreed to participate that evening showed up. It was a testament to how loyal and dedicated our clients were to helping my firm.

After a lovely dinner, we brought in the moderator for the evening. The reason we brought in a moderator was so that I could leave the room and my clients could answer all of the questions honestly. Our questions included "What has your experience been with the firm? How has it been differ-ent from your experience with other firms? What types of communications do you read? Are we delivering the types of services that you want? Are we responding to your needs? What services do you like, or dislike?"

A week later I received the compilation of notes from the moderator and was very pleased to find out that, as a general rule, we were on "the same page" with our clients. They felt we were listening to them and delivering the types of solutions they were looking for. There was one aspect of our role with them that they thought was unique, and brought tremendous value to them and their family: our process that we call our Financial Organizer System.

For many years we "talked" about coordinating our clients' financial information. We had them bring in all of their documents, reviewed them, and made sure we were familiar with them. However, I always felt there was one more step we could take to help our clients and their families. And three years ago we initiated the process of the Financial Organizer System.

The Financial Organizer System has truly helped our clients and their families at levels that go well beyond just the planning issues alone. For example, let's address how most of us "coordinate" our financial affairs. If you are like me, you have "that" closet, with "that" shelf. Whenever financial documents come in the mail we put these documents on the shelf. The pile grows as the years go on, mostly filled with insurance "stuff" and other pertinent documents. We sort of know where everything is — we kind of know what we own — but it really doesn't provide us with a warm and friendly feeling that if the "what if" happens we will be able to find something quickly.

I was actually the first of my clients to initiate the system. I brought in the two feet of papers that had amassed in my closet on "that" shelf and started the process of going through every document. I separated the documents into various piles to first determine what was tax related, investment related, insurance related and other.

I then identified the paperwork that was old and unnecessary and shredded it. This process of shredding, alone, accounted for about 70% of the paperwork that had been on that shelf. The paperwork that was remaining was divided into several categories that had been created in the leather-bound book that evolved into my Financial Organizer.

The first section of the book is for emergency contacts. The first page within this section is a checklist to help the family in the event

You can find this checklist on our website (see introduction for details).

The Financial Organizer System

This system will not only help you to coordinate all of your pertinent financial documents; it can also become a valuable family resource.

The headings to use in your system can include the following:

- Emergency Contacts
- Insurance
- Estate Plan
- Investments
- Charitable Giving Plan
- Bank Documents
- Tax Documents
- Titles & Deeds
- Warranties & Contracts
- Other

of the death of a family member. We included this because the death of a family member is traumatic enough, and we hoped to put the remaining family members on track to be able to do what was necessary, without having to think too much during a very emotional time.

Also included in the first section is a page indicating all the important contact people and a listing of all of life's important documents. This listing breaks down every potential financial or life document that you may own, who provided it to you, where it is located and how long to retain it.

The next several sections break out the investments, estate plan, bank documents, tax information, titles and deeds, warranties and contracts, and other. Once you have coordinated all of the paperwork and placed all of the documents in their respective sections, you have a living, breathing financial organizer.

We then take this to the next level for our clients: We actually scan the contents to their password-protected investment website. The reason we do this is that the benefits of coordinating everything into the system go well beyond just "coordinating paperwork." The system becomes a valuable resource for both our clients and their family members for many years to come.

Let me share with you some of the benefits of this level of coordination. Many of our clients travel; that is actually one of their most common retirement goals. One of my clients was in Europe, got pickpocketed, and lost everything. He went to the nearest cyber-cafe, logged on to his investment website and accessed his Financial Organizer System, and was able to contact all of his credit card companies and alert them to the situation. Very quickly he was able to move from a panic mode, to a feeling of being in control.

As I mentioned, I was the first of my clients to move forward with the system. What I found interesting when I completed the process was I felt more in control than I had ever been, because I knew exactly what I owned and where it was. I was also able to connect some dots that I could not previously, because before, I really didn't know what I owned.

When I actually took a look at the details of my life insurance policy, I found out that the insurance company had changed four times. I still had the same life insurance policy but it had been with four different insurance companies over the past 15 years. So the question is — when I die, will my beneficiaries know who to call? What is most interesting about this question is that many of the estate planning attorneys I work with say that they are constantly chasing the issue of life insurance for their clients. They never seem to really know how much life insurance there is, how many policies there are, and what is actually owned.

I proceeded to contact the most recent insurance company and get a certificate of endorsement indicating they were the company du jour. I also placed in the insurance section a copy of the beneficiary page and a letter indicating that this policy had originally been owned by a different insurance company. In doing so, my beneficiaries will know exactly what to do when I pass.

Another one of my clients brought "the pile of stuff" to our office. When we were sorting through all of the documents, we came across two credit union statements from accounts that had been opened many years ago. My client was actually unaware that he owned these accounts, and as a result "found" $50,000 he didn't know he had.

An even more important benefit is what it does for the family upon the death of one of its members. How often have we heard the story of a family member who took weeks, even months, to go through the attic, the dresser drawers, the checkbook and all of the paperwork in the house to compile what was actually owned? This, during a time of tremendous emotional distress, is not a task easily undertaken.

By having sorted and organized all of the financial data and documents with the Financial Organizer System, that task has been already accomplished. One of my dear clients passed away two years ago, while we were in the midst of putting together his system. His son had to come up from Virginia and spend three weeks away from his family to complete this task. My hope is that we can avoid this for the rest of our clients.

Integrating the Retirement Roadmap and the Financial Organizer System should help you to address most of the issues that you will face in retirement, financial and otherwise. Once you complete this process you should find, as most of my clients do, that you are in more control of your financial affairs than you have ever been before. And by doing so you should be much closer to that peace of mind that you so richly deserve.

CHAPTER 4

WHAT ABOUT WOMEN?

WHAT ARE THE PARTICULAR ISSUES THEY NEED TO ADDRESS?

I think it is important at this time to revisit the three big questions that I believe are the most important issues when it comes to financial planning. First, how do I take care of myself and my spouse so that we can best enjoy our journey? Second, when I die will my spouse be taken care of (actuarial tables tell us that not only does "he" die first, but various studies show that she typically outlives him by 17 years)? Third, how do I make sure that my kids are all set?

So if we assume that the wife is going to outlive the husband, would you not assume that she will be pushing hard for a plan that will take care of her and her kids? Interestingly, studies show that women actually lag men when it comes to taking control of the financial planning process.

In Susan Hirschman's book *Does This Make My Assets Look Fat? A Woman's Guide to Finding Financial Empowerment and Success*, she begins her book by noting three trends in the world of personal finance:

- Investment markets and products are becoming ever more complex;
- An increasing number of women are controlling more and more of the wealth in America. It is estimated that in the very near future women will control at least 60% of the wealth; and
- Women's level of financial literacy is *not* increasing.

Hirschman gives four main reasons as to why women shy away from expanding their financial knowledge:

- They have neither the time nor the inclination;
- It's too overwhelming — and they'll never know everything, so why bother?
- They are embarrassed to let anyone see their lack of knowledge; and
- They assume that their husbands (or fathers or partners) will take care of it for them.

I would like to share with you my perspective regarding women and financial planning. There has been a disconnect between what women need and what the investment community has offered. Why is that, and how can it be corrected? I would like to share some strategies that could help women take more control of their financial affairs.

What Makes Me an Expert?

Some people think that only a woman can provide financial planning advice to women. The reality is that I will never truly be able to feel what they feel or think the way women think. However, I have spent many years learning to communicate (listen) and continue to get better at it. This process of understanding the differences has occurred over many years, and much of that credit goes to my daughter, Erica. In order to "be on the same page" with her, I have had to constantly improve my listening skills. I have learned more from her than any business conference I have attended.

From a professional perspective, almost one-third of our new clients are women who are in transition, either widowed or divorced. I believe that this speaks to the approach that we take with our clients. I believe, first and foremost, that a financial planner must be a good listener, which then helps the planner engage in a healthy, long-term relationship.

Interestingly, the process that we have developed with the Retirement Roadmap is not very different from the roadmap we develop for our women in transition. If you think about it, retirement planning is about setting the stage for what you want to do in the next chapter of your life. The pre-retiree has worked for the past 40 years and wishes to establish those things that are important for the next 25 to 30 years and must, therefore, put in place a plan to accomplish specific goals.

This process of transition is similar to the transition that we talk about with women who are going through a divorce or who have been recently widowed. They are entering a new chapter of life where they need to establish what is important to them and how they wish to lead the rest of their lives. The roadmap helps them to understand these goals and how to accomplish them.

I recently brought on a new client who had been divorced,

officially, for only six months. She had relied on her husband for all of the planning, and when he left her, she was left feeling helpless. She was unsure of how to create the income she needed to live on, and fearful of taking on the task of investing her money. She was scared.

We met four times in the first three months, each meeting lasting about two hours. The most important issue for her was the decision about where to live. She did not have enough assets to buy a home, so she went looking for a proper rental. She thought that she could afford a monthly rental of about $1500 and went searching for units that were in that range. Unfortunately, after several visits with different real estate brokers, she was unable to come up with a unit that was suitable.

We went back to the drawing board, reevaluated her income needs, and found a way for her to increase the monthly allotment for rent up to $2200. She was able to find a rental in that range that was what she wanted.

It was important that I was on the same page with her, to listen to what she wanted, and to create the solution that helped her to take the first step toward taking control of her life.

The Disconnect between Women and the Financial Planning Community

In a recent article written by Olivia Mellan in *Investment Advisor*, she states that "studies continue to show that women are less financially confident than men, despite decades of effort put into making them more comfortable with money and investing."

In that same article, Olivia interviewed a financial planner who was sharing her thoughts about women and investing. This planner had just spoken in front of a number of women who were all professors and elected officials. These women were all in a position of authority and responsibility. She was stunned, at the end of her presentation on the nuts and bolts of charitable giving, that the questions all seemed to revolve around their personal issues with regard to financial planning. Instead of asking technical questions about the topic at hand, the women were asking "How do I find a financial planner?" and "How do I talk to my parents about money?" They were asking the planner "Where do I go?" and "What do I do?" The planner noted that they seemed to be stuck at the very beginning of the process.

There is no doubt that the investment community has been attempting to reach out to women for many years, but the message does not seem to be reaching its intended audience. The reason for the disconnect, I believe, is that the advice is driven by a community that is predominantly male and investment oriented, and continues to communicate in the manner that has made "them" successful.

Men often think of investing in terms of winners and losers, while women think of investing not as a game but rather as a route to sustaining basic financial goals such as funding their child's college education. We, as an industry, must change the way we think about the process of planning and investing if we are to improve the connection with the women whom we are trying to reach.

A perfect example of this disconnect is the story of a client who has been widowed for seven years. When I first met Joan two years ago, she was still feeling very vulnerable. She had lost her husband of 30 years and was now being retired, involuntarily. She was feeling very out of control.

In our first meeting together, she shared with me a story that was very revealing. She told me that her husband's prized possession was his 20-year-old BMW. She did not know very much about the car, and had to take it in to get serviced every once in a while. She told me that each time she took it in for service she left enraged. She felt the service people, all males, were talking down to her and not engaging her as an intelligent human being. She told me the toughest thing that she had to do after her husband's death was to sell that BMW. She no longer wanted to be treated in such a demeaning way.

This theme is repeated over and over again during my conversations with my female clients. They share with me that they did not feel that their previous advisor connected with them. The communications were typically driven by what the advisor wanted to sell, versus uncovering what she was feeling. This was particularly true if they were married at the time of the previous relationship with the advisor.

Few advisors actually take the time to listen to both the husband and the wife. I have always said that a good financial planner is really 50% planner and 50% psychiatrist. It is important not only to recognize the differences in how we process information, but to deliver solutions in a way that they each understand, in their own way.

The Three Biggest Mistakes Financial Advisors Make

I believe there are three big mistakes financial advisors make when working with women.

The first mistake is not understanding how to create a relationship. Most financial advisors were educated in the male-dominated investment industry and were taught how to put together a solid investment portfolio. They would often talk "down" to their female client, particularly if the advisor felt the client was not knowledgeable in the ways of the investment world. Rarely did they take the time to cultivate a relationship — they were too busy managing money.

The successful advisor spends the time to educate their female clients and create unique solutions to fit the particular circumstances for each individual. This entails not only educating the client on the plusses and minuses of each option, but also following through and continuing communication after the decision is made to make sure there is a complete understanding.

The second mistake is not understanding what a newly divorced or widowed woman needs. Many financial advisors get paid solely on managing money. Whether it is a percentage of assets or a commission-based model, most jump at the opportunity immediately to "touch the money." For the recently widowed or divorced woman, this is a huge mistake. After such a life-altering event it is important to let life settle. It is crucial to the success of the long-term emotional and financial well-being for a woman to get grounded, at some level, before moving on to make important decisions such as those dealing with money.

The advisor who takes the time to help the client get through the transition of becoming widowed or divorced, and does not immediately focus on "the money," will have set the foundation for a truly rewarding, long-term relationship.

The third mistake is not understanding how to listen to their female clients.

Many years ago, when Erica was seven, I learned a valuable lesson. She would come to me when she was supposed to take a bath and ask if she should wash her hair. "Of course you should wash your hair," I would say, and World War III would break out. It was not a fun conversation. So one day I tried a different tactic — when she came to me with the same question, I told her she did not have to wash her hair that night. Interestingly, she went ahead and washed it anyway. The lesson: She truly wasn't asking if she should wash her hair, she just wanted to know if she had the choice to do it. So often my female clients ask questions in an effort to gather intelligence, and hearing what they are truly asking is important in order to respond properly.

What is interesting is to understand how far beyond just investment and financial planning issues the relationship can go, once a proper connection is made. One of my long-time clients and I were wrapping up one of our annual review sessions when she started to share with me a situation she was troubled by, and needed to come up with a suitable solution.

Judy is very close to her sister who lives on the West Coast. Her sister had been sick for several years, and it appeared that recently she had started to go downhill. Judy desperately wanted to visit her. The problem was that Judy's partner had some physical limitations. This meant that if Judy were to go visit her sister, she would have to leave her partner, who could not take care of himself. In order to leave, Judy would have had to hire help, which was very expensive and not within their budget. So Judy was stuck trying to come up with a solution.

We talked for some time about the dynamics of her family, both here and on the West Coast. Fortunately, we were able to come up with a solution that seemed to suit Judy's needs: Her sister lived in close proximity to other family members. It was agreed that one of the family members would go visit the sister and bring with them their computer. At the agreed-upon time, her sister would call Judy via the Internet tool Skype, and they would be able to both communicate and see each other.

This solution had nothing to do with financial planning, yet it had everything to do with providing peace of mind for Judy. When we all do a better job of listening, we can attend to the needs of our clients in a way that is far beyond just the investment or retirement decisions.

Estate Planning Considerations for Women

Let us assume for a moment that "she" will outlive "him" and will be left with the task of preserving and protecting their assets for the rest of her life, and also taking care of the proper distribution of assets for her children upon her death.

The process of estate planning is about putting in place the proper documentation so that the caregivers and heirs will know exactly what to do and when. It is important to put these instructions in writing.

Women simply need more money. On average, women live longer than men, and they are more likely to be widowed. Women are often paid less in wages and typically work fewer years than men, resulting in lower Social Security and employer-provided benefits. It is important to acknowledge these facts when working with an estate planning attorney, in order to tailor the planning accordingly.

Two key areas to review are *life insurance* and the *spouse's pension plan.* It is important to understand the impact of the death of the husband on the ability for the surviving spouse to continue to lead her life in the way that she chooses. Often this means that there is a need to develop a properly designed life insurance program. The life insurance proceeds can provide needed liquidity and income that would be necessary to sustain her cash flow needs. However, it is important to own the insurance properly so that it is not unnecessarily taxed upon receipt.

The husband's pension often comes with choices. Assuming he dies first, the surviving spouse may be left with less income, depending upon the pension choice that was taken upon his retirement. It is important to recognize what the choices are and to pick the right pension option in order to make sure that both spouses will be taken care of.

Women often have an interest in charitable giving. For many women, charitable giving is a key estate planning goal, providing both emotional and financial benefits. It is necessary to take the time to develop a plan that balances charitable giving with asset preservation and retirement income planning.

Women's needs are often defined by their marital status. Married, single and previously married women have different estate planning needs, as do women with blended families. Married women should be encouraged to take an equal role in the estate planning process to ensure that their future needs are met.

Women in second marriages or with blended families may be particularly concerned with children's needs, as well as protecting their individual interests. Planning is no less important for single women, who may wish to provide for their parents, siblings or children.

Open communication is truly the key to putting in place a proper estate plan. As a Certified Financial Planner®, I typically initiate the conversation about estate planning with my client, and then direct her to see the proper estate planning attorney. It is important for the dialogue to be open and honest, and it must touch on topics well beyond the usual financial conversations. Understanding the relationships within the family is an important element to crafting a successful estate plan.

Once you have completed the estate planning process, you should feel more secure, organized and aware about your future and that of your surviving heirs. This will help you achieve the peace of mind you so richly deserve. An important note to keep in mind is that as your life changes, or your goals change, you should revisit the estate planning documents to make sure they are reflective of your current wishes.

Steps to Strengthening Your Financial Position

Here is a five-step process to help put you take more control of your financial life. I have used this process to help my female clients who are in transition.

First, *make the time*. Women typically are better at multitasking than are men, and this is both a good and bad characteristic. The good news is that women are dealing with many issues and are often able to accomplish more than men. The downside to multitasking is that life may feel a bit chaotic, and it may be difficult to sit down and focus on one particular issue clearly.

My recommendation is to make financial planning a high priority in your life and to clear your calendar, be it for an hour or for a day, to focus on this important aspect of your life.

Second, *paint your picture*. Most coaches, personal or professional, will tell you that the best way to accomplish your goals is to actually visualize where it is you want to end up and how you want to get there. How do you want to live the rest of your life? What is most important to you? What do you want to accomplish?

This exercise can be daunting, because it is difficult to visualize what you truly want to do or what you want to become 10, 20 or even 30 years from now. So I suggest to start thinking about what you want to accomplish over the next two or three years. In that way it becomes a much more manageable exercise. This will be the start of your Bucket List. The Bucket List can include trips you would like to go on, relationships you would like to improve upon, adventures you would like to start, or any other items of importance to you. Make this Bucket List as personal as you can.

Third, *put a plan in place*. Once you've established what it is you wish to accomplish, put it in writing. I am a big believer in delegating and utilizing experts who are available to help me accomplish my goals. Therefore, if your life is constantly busy and you are often on the go, hiring a financial planner may be one of the best decisions you can make.

Think of your financial planner as your coach. You will want to develop an open and trusting relationship with this individual. Your planner needs to understand what keeps you up at night, and what you wish to accomplish for the rest of your life. The financial planner should help ease the burden of your day-to-day decision-making and enable you to focus in on the other areas of your life. By aligning your interests with a qualified financial planner, you will have a guide to lean on to help you enjoy your retirement journey.

Fourth, *become financially organized*. After you have written your plan, it is time to get rid of some of the clutter that you may be dealing with as a result of all of the paperwork that will be coming your way. One of the tools that we use with our clients is our Financial Organizer System that is referenced in Chapter 3.

The Financial Organizer System will ultimately not only put you in more control of the overwhelming amount of paper that you will be receiving, but also provide a resource for you and your entire family to deal with all of your pertinent financial data. A benefit of being in control and more organized is that you will be able to focus on other areas of your life, knowing that you have taken care of this one.

Fifth, *enjoy your life*. My philosophy (and my e-mail address) is to "enjoy the journey." Given what comes at us on a day-to-day basis, sometimes it is difficult to truly enjoy the journey that we are on. Every once in a while we have to just step back and take a proper perspective on what it is we've accomplished in life and how blessed we are.

Even in the midst of your busy day, try to find a moment to step back and gain that proper perspective, or view that wonderful sunset, that can bring joy to your life. And part of the joy of having put together a successful financial plan is that you know that you are taking care of yourself and your family. But the work is not done.

It is important to put a tickler in on a semiannual basis to review your goals and to make sure that your plan is updated. The more you stay on top of your plan, the better the chance you will have of truly enjoying your journey into retirement.

CHAPTER 5
DECIDING NOT TO GO IT ALONE
CHOOSING A FINANCIAL PLANNER

Let's assume that if you've gotten this far, you are truly interested in the concept of financial planning. So the real question becomes, how do you put together a plan for yourself? And where do you go for the advice to put a plan together that reflects the wants and needs for the rest of your life?

There was a television commercial that showed a man at a table. He was shirtless, and had a knife in one hand and the phone in the other. He was asking the person on the phone to guide him through the necessary steps so that he could perform open-heart surgery on himself.

Now I am not suggesting that the process of financial planning is as complex as open-heart surgery. What I am suggesting, though, is that there are people who would like to do everything on their own. There are certain tasks in life that you can do on your own: You don't need a mechanic to change the oil in your car. You don't need a carpenter to build shelves in your closet. You don't need a travel agent to build your itinerary for your upcoming trip. You could accomplish these tasks, along with many others, either by doing it on your own or by using an expert.

I submit, however, that there are some tasks for which you must use an expert. So the question about financial planning is, do you need to use an expert? Or, to ask the question a different way, will using a financial professional bring you closer to accomplishing your financial dreams than if you just did it on your own? In this chapter I will teach you how to think through the process of whether or not it is in your best interests to hire a financial planner, and if so, how to do that.

What Are You Looking for?

Every industry must recognize the wants and needs of its potential customer base. The financial services industry is no different. There are volumes upon volumes of studies that have been done so that "we" know what "you" are looking for. What is important to you in your search to gain financial freedom? What are you looking for, in a financial services professional, to help you to accomplish your goals?

In a recent study by The Oechsli Institute, affluent investors were interviewed in order to gain insights into how they were thinking about their financial affairs. A portion of the study, published in 2010, centered on what was rated as "very important" by this group of investors.

Here is that list of items:

1. Provide clear and timely communication
2. Resolve problems quickly and to my satisfaction
3. Be focused on overseeing my family's financial affairs, not marketing his/her practice
4. Meet my investment performance expectations
5. Possess a comprehensive breadth and depth of industry knowledge
6. Always have my family's best interests behind every financial recommendation
7. Fully disclose all fees
8. Keep me informed of any events that might impact my family's finances
9. Deliver high-level personal service
10. Care more about me than just my investments
11. Fully understand my family's goals and needs
12. Help me create and execute a formal financial plan
13. Develop and communicate a financial recovery strategy for my family
14. Coordinate all of my family's investment decisions
15. Help me organize and keep up-to-date all my important financial documents
16. Use outside experts to help with other financial areas

As you take a look at the list above, there are some important themes to recognize. First, as I've referenced throughout this book, the focus should be on the total picture, not primarily on the investment portfolio. This study echoes earlier studies showing that the conversation about investments is not *the* driving force behind what the affluent investor is looking for. Additionally, as you look through the list, only two of the 16 characteristics have anything to do with investments.

Second, communication is the key to a successful relationship. This should be no surprise, for whether you are talking about the relationship with your spouse, your kids or your peers, or the prospective relationship with a financial planner, clear communication is the foundation of any successful relationship. Being "on the same page" is a very important consideration when entertaining the idea of hiring a financial planner.

Third, coordination/organization of the family's affairs is a high priority. Several of the characteristics in the list deal with properly understanding the *total* picture for the family.

Finally, the ability to recognize issues, and then solve problems in a timely fashion, is a key characteristic of what the affluent investor is looking for.

Another part of the study was entitled "Top Reasons Clients Leave Advisers." The previous list indicated what the Bucket List is for affluent investors who are looking for a relationship with a financial advisor. This study, on the other hand, details the most frequent reasons why the relationship between the financial advisor and a client breaks down.

Here is a list of those reasons:

- Repeated mistakes by advisor and/or team
- Too focused on marketing, not enough on family's financial affairs
- Poor communication
- Does not trust the stability of his or her firm
- Lack of transparency with fees
- Investment performance not meeting expectations

This list is interesting in that it incorporates some old, and some new, issues.

As you can see in the list, investment performance is typically *not* the driving force behind the breakdown of the relationship between the financial planner and his/her client. Poor communication and the inability to maintain the client at the center of the relationship usually are at the top of the lists.

Two of the bullet points are reflective of more recent fears driven by the headlines of our times.

First, we are living in the post-Bernie Madoff era. Investors are demanding more and more fully-disclosed reporting of the fees associated with their investments.

Second, as a result of the recent financial meltdown and the impact on some of the major brokerage houses, many individuals need more assurances that the organization and the people that they are dealing with are trustworthy. No longer is it good enough just to have a name that has been in the industry for many decades.

An example of this is a conversation I had with a client. We were talking about his experience with my firm and how his experience compared to his friends' experiences with their financial planners. My client had been under the impression that since his friends had financial planners, they were "all set," but when he drilled down a little deeper he learned otherwise. Some of his friends indicated that their current planners had been "all over them" when they first brought the money over. Now that the relationship with their planners had been going on for several years, they found that the relationship, or as they put it, "the communication level," had changed. His friends, he found out, were actually looking for new financial planners, not because of poor performance per se, but because they felt they were no longer important to the financial planner.

I have heard it many times in my 25 years — it is not the investment performance that drives people away, it is the lack of attention they are given.

Do-It-Yourselfers

Through the years I have had the opportunity, through the television or radio shows I produced or various speaking engagements, to speak with many people. In no particular order, the four most common reasons I have heard over the years as to why they would not hire a financial planner are 1) fear/trust, 2) cost/expense, 3) privacy and 4) lack of understanding of what a planner does.

So let's start with the fear/trust issue. I referenced earlier in this chapter the post-Madoff era and its impact on our industry. In normal times it can be very difficult to gain someone's trust or overcome their fear when it comes to dealing with money. The recent headlines have served to fuel the issues of fear and trust even for those who had never been fearful before.

I completely understand the emotions that many people are dealing with and how hesitant they might be to engage someone in our industry. The best advice I can give someone is to do as much research as possible, and talk to as many people as possible, in order to come up with someone that you feel you can work with and generate a trusting relationship with over time.

The issue of cost, or expense, is an interesting one. I hear two different takes on this. First, there are some people for whom, at any cost, hiring a professional is too much. For those people, it is better for them to do it on their own. They will not have a happy relationship, no matter what is done for them — it is better for them, and for the planner, to not move forward with a relationship.

Then there are those who want to get value for what they pay. I think of it as a simple proposition — if you think a professional can add value for you, you should hire him/her. He/she will get paid in some form, be it a commission or a fee, and you have to determine if what he/she is charging seems fair in light of the value he/she is offering.

I have always made the analogy that you can do your own taxes. However, if I hire an accountant who costs me $500 to do a return and he finds $1000 worth of tax deductions that I could not find on my own, he was worth the $500. The same formula holds true when considering hiring a financial planner. If the planner can add value, then they are worth the expense.

The issue of privacy is an interesting one. There are people who would much prefer that no one ever know what they own, how they own it, or how much they are worth. I understand and respect this. However, that person may be leaving their heirs in a bad situation.

Many years ago I had a client who was in his early 50s. His father, who was still working at the firm that he had built, was 92 years old. The father was worth somewhere between $5 and $7 million and did not want anyone to provide him with any advice. Unfortunately, upon his death, because there was no planning done in advance, most of the real estate had to be liquidated and the net proceeds available to the son were a little less than $1 million.

I believe that if the father knew that he had squandered over $5 million as a result of not moving forward with any planning, he would be turning over in his grave.

The last item, a lack of understanding, is quite common. I do not believe that our industry has done a good job of helping the public understand exactly what a "planner" does. There are so many people who use the word "advisor" or "planner" that it can be difficult to differentiate who does what. To overcome this lack of understanding, I provide in this chapter some of the questions you should ask to determine what the prospective planner does or does not do for their clients. It is important to find someone who is a good "fit" for you, and the burden is on you to ask the right questions.

It has been my experience that even self-professed do-it-yourselfers find that there are times when they feel it is important to engage a financial planner. There are two circumstances that seem to cause these people to seek advice.

The first situation is a do-it-yourselfer who has been managing the money on his own and feels he has been doing a very good job. But as he gets older, he does not feel he has the time or temperament to continue to manage all of the money. It is at this time of his life that he moves forward to bring on a planner to manage all or a part of the money.

The second situation is one where a person has been managing the financial affairs for the family forever. There usually comes a time when he understands that upon his death he will be leaving his affairs to his wife, who is not familiar with how to deal with finances. He realizes the importance of creating a relationship before he is gone, so that his surviving spouse can have somebody by her side during a very difficult time of her life. It is not wise to have the spouse look for a planner, someone she can trust, just at the time of his death. It is better to have the relationship already established.

Different Types of Planning Models

It is important for you to understand how the financial planning industry has evolved and the different types of planning models that are available to you.

The industry has been focused on attracting people who have money, so that we can manage that money and get paid for doing so. Also, the industry's general focus on investments is a major reason why most people only think of money management when they think of "planning." Over the years, however, the definition of planning has evolved and it now encompasses much more than just investments.

So let's take a look at four of the different types of financial professionals that profess to do planning, and how they get paid. These four different types are insurance agents, accountants, traditional brokers and independent financial planners.

Life insurance agents have been around forever. Historically, their primary product was some form of life insurance that was commission-based. Several years ago the insurance companies recognized that they were leaving a lot of money on the table, and decided it was important for their life insurance agents to become better-rounded.

Many of today's life insurance agents now focus on both the sale of life insurance and the sale of investment-oriented products. Typically they have available to them the proprietary products associated with the insurance company that they are working for. Life insurance agents provide an excellent insurance platform for their clients, while trying to add value to their clients' investment portfolios.

The accounting industry, as a whole, tried to make changes to their business models about 12 to 15 years ago. They, too, recognized that they were leaving a lot of money on the table by "just" doing the accounting for their clients. So many accountants decided to add financial planning to their menu of services. The changes came in two forms.

The majority of the accountants that I have spoken with tried to do financial planning on their own, in addition to tax work. As a general rule, they recognized that they were not able to wear all of the hats necessary in an effort to add financial planning, and had to rethink how they were going to bring financial planning (or if they should) to their clients.

The accounting firms who were successful in making this model change typically were those who brought in experienced financial planners to do the work for their clients. These firms approached financial planning in its truest sense and were compensated through either a fee or a commission for their work.

The traditional broker is what most of the retail clientele think of when they think of financial planning. These brokers are typically employed by large, well-known financial institutions, and their educational background is usually centered on portfolio management. Traditionally they were paid a commission for each transaction they generated for the client, be it a stock or bond trade or the sale of a mutual fund type of product.

This model has evolved as well, and many of the large brokerage firms are offering their version of financial planning for a fee. The assets-under-management model, where the planner gets paid an annual fee to manage the money, has become the platform of choice. There are still traditional brokers who work on a transaction-to-transaction basis; however, more and more brokers are embracing the assets-under-management fee model.

Finally, there are the independent financial planners. These financial planners do not have managers telling them what to sell; they are making their own decisions. The more successful and mature financial planning firms who are associated with the larger independent broker-dealers can offer an enormous selection of investment products to their clients.

It is typically within the world of independent financial planners that you would find true planners. These individuals are focused on providing complete financial planning to clients, well beyond just the investment-related products that the other sectors of the industry are providing. These days many independent financial planners now get paid in two different ways: They charge a fee to put together a plan, and also a fee to manage the money. Some still provide commission-based products to their clients. The independent financial planner typically has a more consultative approach than a product sales approach.

I am an independent financial planner. I do have a bias in terms of what I believe is the best model, and that is the model that I have been providing my clients for 25 years as a Certified Financial Planner®. I also recognize the benefit of having different models.

Just as Baskin Robbins has 31 different flavors, our industry needs to offer different flavors to our potential customers. I may like Chunky Monkey, where someone else may like Butter Pecan, so it is important to have a flavor that matches each customer. The same holds true in our industry.

The most important thing to remember is that there are different ways to provide "financial planning," and the burden is on you to make sure that you are aligning yourself with the professional and the approach that are right for you.

The Interview Process

I believe a good relationship is based on solid communication and trust. The corollary is that when the communication process breaks down, there is a high probability that there will be a strain on the relationship.

You can find a list to prepare you for your interview on our website (see introduction for details).

The foundation for a good relationship with a financial planner starts at the beginning, by understanding what the expectations are. Let's go back to the analogy with the medical community — if you are looking for a heart surgeon, you are in the wrong place if you are talking to a general practitioner. *So the very first thing that you have to define is what you are looking for, and what you want the results to be.*

These are my "expectations" when I am talking to a prospective client: that they will be forthcoming and honest with me about both financial and emotional needs — if I don't know everything that I can about my client, then I cannot possibly provide a solution that is suitable for the client. So my expectation is that there will be "active" participation between the client and myself.

I share with prospective clients what they can expect from

Questions You Should Ask When Interviewing a Planning Firm

- Who are their clients?
- What is their area of expertise?
- What is the planner's background/experience?
- How is this advisor compensated?
- Who employs the advisor?
- Who controls/has access to the money?
- What kind of ongoing service does the advisor provide?
- What is the planner's mission statement?

me and my firm. I tell them I will work diligently to listen to what their particular issues are in order to come up with customized solutions for their particular situation. I tell them that there will be numerous ongoing communications from our firm, on a number of different levels, in an effort to keep our clients fully informed. The information and communications that we disseminate could range from general tax law changes to very specific recommendations for the client's Retirement Roadmap.

We even go so far as to make one to two calls a year to each client just to see how he is doing. It may be that since we last met there was a change in his life that has not yet been shared with us. By being proactive with our communication process, we can be on the same page with our clients.

This type of information is necessary to gather during the initial interview, because you want to make sure you have the right fit. For example, if a prospective client is interviewing me and my firm and they would prefer to remain very private with their information, or have no desire to participate actively with us, then that prospect may not be a good fit for my firm. Both the prospect and the planning firm must understand each other's expectations, or the relationship will more than likely falter.

Here are some of the questions you should ask in order to assess whether a planning firm is a good fit for you:

Who are their clients?

It is important to understand the type of individual the advisor normally works with. Again, you wouldn't go to an eye specialist if you just broke your arm. The same is true with money; you want someone who is conversant with your particular issues.

What is their area of expertise?

As I mentioned earlier in this chapter, there are different types of people that you can seek out depending upon what your issues are. If you are looking to purchase life insurance, you should probably go to a life insurance agent. If you are looking for college planning advice, you should go to somebody who specializes in college planning. If you are looking for retirement plan advice, you should go to somebody who specializes in the transition into retirement.

It is important, when asking questions about the planner's expertise, to have the planner give you some hypothetical scenarios that they have been involved with. If they say that they can help you with your college planning issues, then they should be able to, off the top of his or her head, offer stories about providing that specific advice to their clients. They should be able to share with you exactly how they walk through the process of providing the specific solutions that you are looking for.

What is the planner's background/experience?

My standards when I look for an expert are very high. I want someone who has been around for many years, seen many different things, and been through both good and bad times. Within the world of financial planning, I believe you should align yourself with someone who has been in the business at least 10 to 15 years and holds the designation of Certified Financial Planner®. The CFP® designation is one of the most highly regarded designations in the field of financial planning. It represents a commitment to the industry and to the planner's educational background that is important if you are looking for the best.

How is this advisor compensated?

As I have outlined earlier in this chapter, there are different ways that advisors can get paid in our industry. Generally, financial planners are paid either by fees only, commissions only, or a hybrid of fees and commissions. Much is written about the "best" approach, but what is more important is how the approach benefits you. No one way is best. You are going to pay for hiring a professional, so select a way that is most comfortable for you.

Who employs the advisor?

It is incumbent upon you to recognize any hidden agendas. If the advisor works for one of the large firms, there is a chance that your portfolio will eventually be made up of many of their proprietary products. It only makes sense for them to push the products the company benefits from. If the advisor is independent, you'll probably be able to choose from a wider selection of investment choices.

This is not to say that one approach is better than another; it just is a matter of recognizing what will transpire, and what to expect. If you are expecting an objective view toward money, you need to know what the perspective of your advisor is. Additionally, if the advisor is hired by a major company, the marketing department may provide all advisors with the title of "financial planner" — it is more user-friendly than "investment advisor" or "insurance agent." *A true planner has earned the designation, not just been given the title as a marketing tool.*

Who controls/has access to the money?
This gets back to the recent post-Madoff era headlines and the potential that someone could possibly "take" your money. You need to find out how the money gets moved, by whom, and to whom the checks are written. There are actually very few instances of advisors running away with clients' money, yet they always hit the front pages. Just be careful.

What kind of ongoing service does the advisor provide?
The best way to maintain a valued client is to provide ongoing communication and a high level of service. Not all advisors put an emphasis on this — many just pay lip service. If it is important to you, ask what kind of service you can expect. If it is appropriate, ask to see the communications the planner has provided to current clients.

What is the planner's mission statement?
You want an advisor who can clearly communicate what his

business does and who it serves. If it is clear to you where the business is going and what it does, then you have increased the chance your advisor will be able to communicate clearly with you about your needs.

This also gives you an opportunity to better understand if there is a proper fit. If a prospective client was to come into my office and interview me and ask me, "What is your mission statement?" I would tell him that I specialize in retirement planning and helping women who are in transition. If he/she is looking for life insurance or college planning, then he/she would know right off the bat that my firm is not the right fit for them.

There is no "best" way to proceed. Each individual has his/her own set of emotional and economic needs. We all have our own comfort levels, and our own expectations as to how issues should be handled. The most important aspect of choosing a financial planner is to find someone with whom you could develop a long-standing, trusting relationship.

Trust does not come overnight, however; it is earned. It is easy for a professional to paint a picture that the prospective client would want to hear. The true measure of whether a professional will be able to be trusted by the prospective client is by making sure that the planner actually delivers, over time, what he said he would at the initial interview.

When considering a financial planner, do all you can to learn as much about them as you can in order to get the best fit for your needs. *The more that you participate in the process, the more you get to know and act in a dual capacity with your planner, the higher the chances you will achieve the financial security you so richly deserve.*

ABOUT THE AUTHOR

Mark Singer is a Certified Financial Planner® practitioner whose career spans 25 years and all kinds of markets. He created the "Retirement Roadmap" and the "Financial Organizer System," both of which have helped thousands of investors successfully coordinate their financial affairs. Mark is also a frequent speaker at events, teaches for the non-profit Heartland Institute as a Certified Financial Educator (CFEd®), and founded the Greater Boston Corporate Wellness Forum. He hosts "Your Financial Future" on Blogtalk Radio and was the host of television's long-running program "Your Money Matters." He has also been the host of "Retirement Corner" on WBOQ 104.9 FM and "Retirement Strategies" on WESX 1230 AM radio.

Over his career Mark has seen just about everything, but he has never before seen as much confusion among investors over financial options — and that's where *The Changing Landscape of Retirement* comes in!

Moving Ahead with Your Retirement Journey...

Book Mark Singer CFP® to present at an upcoming event or workshop by contacting him:

mark@yourretirementjourney.com

781-599-5009

To find out where Mark is speaking next, download free worksheets or have your own personal retirement questions answered, visit him on the web:

www.yourretirementjourney.com